Naked Warriors

Making Disciples by Destroying Isolation

Naked Warriors

Making Disciples by Destroying Isolation

Brian Childres

Table of Contents

Chapter 1: The Power of Unity 7

Chapter 2: Man's Greatest Problem 15

Chapter 3: Invitation of a Lifetime 23

Chapter 4: Rites of Initiation 35

Chapter 5: Priority of the Heart 47

Chapter 6: Being Brothers: Sharpening 57

Chapter 7: Being Brothers: Praying and Affirming 69

Chapter 8: Being Brothers: Repenting 79

Chapter 9: One More Man 87

Chapter 10: How to Change the World 99

Chapter 11: A Simple Challenge 111

Chapter 1

The Power of Unity

I am blessed, having lived all my life in a rural community filled with men who love Jesus. Like many areas, particularly pockets in the South and Midwest, East Texas has a reputation as a peaceful Christian haven, especially compared with other, more conflict-ridden areas of our troubled nation. With more than three hundred churches and some of the largest ministries in the world headquartered here, many of us think of our region as a bit of a "Jesus paradise."

I live in Tyler, where we have some incredibly gifted preachers and teachers. There is no shortage of biblical truth taught here. Any man can walk into most any church on a given Sunday and hear rock-solid Bible teaching. And therein lies our struggle. Our churches have succeeded in producing well-equipped soldiers, but struggle to build a unified army. There is a huge difference between the two. If my hunch is right, your community faces a similar obstacle.

We have thousands of strong, good-hearted Christian men. However, few of those men have been united intimately with other godly men. As a whole, the men in most churches have not been commissioned as a unified platoon outside of the four walls of their churches. So, we have capable soldiers, yet a small army. It is difficult—if not impossible—to win a war without an army. I would rather go into battle on any day with a cohesive squadron of ten soldiers than a thousand individually trained ones.

The United States Army is tremendously effective at building a cohesive unit that can annihilate any enemy. My son is a soldier who has served on active duty with his National Guard unit at the Texas border. He is the first to tell you that the Army's success depends on melding men into an interdependent brotherhood. In the armed forces, there are no individual heroes.

While this book is aimed at the male species, it is not a "Christian manhood" book. There are plenty of those; I enjoy reading books on Christian manhood. But this book does not fall into that category.

I once posed a question to a group of men: "Do you think it is possible to be a godly man?" When all responded in the affirmative, I looked them square in the eye and told them: "It is impossible to be a *godly man*." One older gentleman got rather offended, intensely disagreeing with what he saw as a harsh statement.

In response, I pointed out the key word to my question: *man*.

"There is no such thing as a godly *man*," I explained. "There are only godly *men*."

Think about that for a second. Do you see the profound difference between the two? We are only healthy and powerful when we are *together* as men. God created the body of Christ to live in community. He wants us to live in the plural, as submitted, transparent, vulnerable people. Many of us have been duped into thinking that spiritual growth and discipleship is a personal journey, yet nothing could be further from the truth.

The American phenomena of individualism has infected the church. I watch too many Christians invest enormous amounts of time and energy into spiritual activity that is focused on individual, private spiritual growth. The tech explosion, as personified by YouTube sermons, Facebook worship services, and Christ-centered phone apps, has only added to the struggle. We are never more isolated than when we are staring into our smartphone screen or laptop. We may be fully engaged in "Christian activity" while remaining utterly alone. The hard truth is: my favorite preaching podcast will never be able to look me in the eyes, listen as I confess my sin, and accept me unconditionally.

Wrong Target

Recently, a pastor told me that his goal is for every man in his church to have a daily quiet time of thirty minutes of prayer and Bible reading. He was convinced that if every man got up each morning and devoured the Word of God and prayed, it would transform his church. While I disagreed, I didn't say anything. Unfortunately, I didn't have the courage to inform him that he was aiming at the wrong target. A half-hour prayer time at 5:30 a.m. every day will do nothing to cancel the destructive power of isolation for a man.

Am I refusing to acknowledge the power of consistency in our prayer closet? Not at all. I am simply declaring the insanity of attempting to be spiritually healthy when there is no one in your church who knows the real you. The bottom line is: You CAN'T follow Jesus by yourself! It is impossible to be spiritually healthy if you are not part of an intimate team of godly men. Following Christ by yourself is an impotent religious game, which leads to pain and destruction.

I know. I wasted years in ministry attempting to disciple individual men who had no spiritual brothers in their lives. These great guys kept coming back week after week to meet with me and receive every ounce of ministry I had to offer. Yet, my efforts accomplished few positive results. Why? They were trying to live the Christian life in a vacuum. Without a brotherhood for support, they were doomed to a pattern of failure because no one can go it alone.

So, this book will not tell you how to be a good husband, father, or leader. Many of you reading these words likely know the "how-to" of your roles as a Christian man. As a matter of fact, if you have been a believer for at least a year and attended a Bible-teaching church for most of that time, you have more than enough truth to successfully live the Christian life.

In the pages that follow, I will relate the story of the men's movement in East Texas. Because of men I associate with beyond our area, I know similar grassroots movements are springing up in places like Utah, Arizona, and Oklahoma. As I relate the miracles we have seen over the past decade, I want to relay how you and your church can join this revolution-- no matter where you live.

I say this after watching hundreds of men get initiated into this band of brothers. The result is typically the same: a man's life is transformed, and his family is impacted. This in turn impacts the life of another man, and then another, and another. The primary benefactors in all of this are pastors and the local church.

This men's movement is about more than discipling a group of men; it is creating a healthy, sustainable revival in the local church. Most pastors I know have a burning desire to see increase in solid marriages, healthy children, spiritually robust teens, humble leaders, and strong male participation in congregational life. The only hope for these desires to be fulfilled is a men's relational discipleship movement within local churches.

Now, there is nothing wrong with having a strong marriage ministry, children's program, or youth ministry. It's just that these programs will not produce healthy marriages, children, or teens. This only comes from having a church with a strong foundation of men, intimately connected one to another.

Mutual Rescue

I write this book out of personal gratitude for what the East Texas men's revival has done in my life. Back in 2012, I was struggling during an excruciating season of marriage. The day of my eighteenth anniversary fell on a Tuesday, with the gloomy skies and rain pelting East Texas symbolizing an eight-months-long separation with my wife. Despite our division, I wanted to buy an anniversary card for the woman whom I had loved for so many years.

Stumbling into Walmart as I dodged rain drops, I bought a card, and sprinted back to the car. Then, I made a split-second decision to not give it to her and crammed the card into the glove compartment. The tragedy of not being able to celebrate my marriage on this special day hit me like a sledgehammer, overwhelming me with grief. Soon, I pulled into a convenience store to grab a six-pack of beer and guzzled four of them before I pulled into my driveway.

Turning off the ignition, with the pain of longing and loneliness weighing on me, I burst into tears. As the rain continued to fall, I felt covered by a blanket of despair. Needing to escape, I decided to drive two hours to another city where I could hide in a strip club and get drunk. That was the only plan I could devise to dull the ache inside. As I prepared to set out on my journey, I shot a quick text to Mike, one of my spiritual brothers, reading:

18th Anniversary today. Painful. Pray for me. Much temptation.

Within two minutes he shot back a reply: "I am tempted tonight as well. But I'll stand strong for you brother and pray for you. Know that you are covered."

Something happened in my heart that night as I read my friend's words. But it was more than just his message: it was the love and commitment he expressed, leaving me feeling as if Mike was physically standing by my side. It represented a powerful force—light entering a vast darkness. Even though I was by myself, I was not alone.

Miraculously, instead of driving to the strip club, I went inside and fell sleep. After a peaceful, restful evening, I awoke the next morning and soon received a call from Mike. He confided in me, telling me how he had been in a fierce battle with temptation while on a business trip when he received my text. It moved him to declare that he would take a stand for me and fiercely intercede for my pain and temptation instead of giving in to his own sinful struggle. Because God showed up for both of us, on that rainy Tuesday night, two men rescued one another.

Power of Brotherhood

This is the power of brotherhood. As a result of this movement, I have watched this same miraculous provision and transformation happen hundreds of times in the lives of men like you and me. And I never grow tired of watching it happen. If you are a leader in your church—whether that is as a pastor, deacon, elder, or small group leader—the challenges and truths in this book can change the destiny of your church. I urge you to begin building a band of brothers in your church this week. Don't wait. Start immediately.

My pastor, Pat Alvey, has watched this men's renewal sweep through our church. Not too long ago he remarked, "I have been waiting to see this kind of transformation happen in the lives of men for the past thirty years in ministry." My pastor is no different than you or me. We all long to see a genuine renewal in the body of Christ. If it is a true move of God, then the men of the church will be leading the way.

Wait no longer, my friend. The renewal is full steam ahead! In fact, it has never really slowed down since Jesus began the revolution with His small brotherhood. More churches are jumping into this movement each week. Pastors are realizing that men are not going to commit to a church because the sermons are biblical, the worship is professional, and the coffee is fresh. A cutting-edge website will not disciple the men in your church; the souls of men are crying out loudly for something more. Ordinary men need to embrace the Jesus found in other ordinary men.

As for you and the men in your church, all you need to do is join the revolution. There is no need to linger for God to move, or pray for a fresh vision for the church, or travel somewhere to attend a conference. You don't have to advertise a new men's ministry initiative or order a DVD series. Just grab a couple of men and jump in.

Take a little time so I can relate the story of the East Texas brotherhood, which is the same story being lived by other men in other places as a grassroots men's movement accelerates. But be forewarned, after reading this book you will be armed with more than enough truth to start a revolution in your heart and in your local church. Once you are equipped, you will face a pivotal decision. I hope you will answer in the affirmative. In the meantime, enjoy the journey.

CHAPTER 2

Man's Greatest Problem

The year was 1986. It was a sunny day as my buddies Jim and Chris and I sailed down the highway, all three of us cackled with laughter, optimism, and the freshness of putting last week's high school graduation in the rearview mirror. Hoping to reduce the time needed to make the customary two-hour drive home from our favorite water park, my foot pressed a bit harder on the gas pedal. Suddenly, a mischievous grin crossed Chris's face as he said, "Hey, guys. You have the guts to make a slight detour and pay a visit to the Ponderosa Ranch?"

Jim and I looked at each other with a chuckle and answered in the affirmative. After years of what most folks would call urban legends—tales shared by brave souls who supposedly had taken glimpses of the delights behind this fabled gated community—curiosity had finally gotten the best of us. We were just minutes away from having this burning itch scratched.

Soon we pulled up to a mammoth, tightly shuttered gate. The mere sight of the ominous-looking, wrought-iron obstacle looming over us nearly melted our resolve. The Ponderosa was no ordinary "ranch." It was East Texas's one and only nudist colony. Rolling down the driver's side window, I nervously pushed the intercom button. A cheerful, masculine voice asked how he could help us. Lying, I replied that we were looking to book a place for our upcoming summer vacation. The creaking of the monstrous gate signified that he had bought our story. We were in!

We filled the quarter-mile drive to the main office with adrenaline mixed with flights of fancy and fear that we would be discovered. Our hearts pounded madly as I slowly guided the wheels into a parking spot. We exchanged furtive glances at each other as we walked slowly toward the office's large wooden doors. No turning back now.

While we tried to step confidently into the building, our eyes opened wide at what we saw: a seventy-year-old man wearing nothing but tube socks and sandals. We tried to hide our horror behind masks of nonchalance as we greeted this jovial fellow, who shared enthusiastically about the volleyball tournament and asked, "Do you enjoy horseback riding?"

At that moment, all we could think about was hustling out the same black gate that we had entered. Our testosterone rush had quickly fizzled, and it was time to exit the premises. After we thanked the naked man for his time, he told us to be sure to come out the following month for the crowning of Miss Ponderosa. After speeding away, we laughed all the way home. Fantasy had collided with reality! Needless to say, that was my first and last visit to the Ponderosa Ranch.

The First Nudist Colony

The second chapter of Genesis tells us about the first nudist resort ever built. As a matter of fact, mankind got off to a perfect start living in Eden Ranch, a community full of naked people. Well, two naked people: Adam and Eve. Have you ever considered that God created a nudist colony to be the crowning achievement of His creation?

Scripture utters a profound commentary describing the first man and woman: "Adam and his wife were both naked, and they felt no shame" (Gen. 2:25). Adam and his bride, at least for a short time, were able to experience total freedom. They harbored no shame or embarrassment. No prideful displays or people-pleasing. No striving or condemnation. Nothing but a blissful, innocent, perfect relationship with God and each other. Can you imagine a life like that? It's what every person desires: genuine freedom.

The first man had absolutely nothing to hide. Not even his hairy butt or dangling penis! His physical nakedness was simply an expression of his inner state. His freedom was so complete that he had no awareness of himself. None. His life was consumed with enjoying God, his wife, and all of creation.

Sadly, the fun didn't last long. A single act of sin and the nudist ranch abruptly closed its gates. It's likely you know the story. Before the day ended, Adam learned to sew a loincloth as awareness of sin prevailed and shame set in for the long haul. Genesis 3:10 shows the debilitating cycle that will play over and over for generations to come. God comes looking for Adam, who is crouching in the woods. When he finally gathers enough courage to respond to the question, "Where are you?" Adam admits, "I heard you in the garden, and I was afraid because I was naked; so, I hid."

Sin gave birth to a horrific creation-- a dance we can call "The Three-Step." This pattern remains the great struggle for every Christian man: 1) see our nakedness, 2) become afraid, 3) hide. Every man alive struggles with pain, temptations, and doubt. Since this is an innate part of our God-given humanity, we as men cannot hide from this messy truth. When confronted with reality, we have a choice concerning how we view ourselves: we can choose to see ourselves as naked and unashamed, or not.

Often, we choose to NOT see ourselves as God sees us. Father God declares that as His child you are a worthy, righteous, powerful, loving, and talented man. Do you believe this? There are times in my life when I look at myself and believe something different. I believe the devil's lie about who I am. As a result, I become ashamed.

According to Genesis 3:10, this first step (shame) causes the second step: a reflex response called fear. We become afraid. Have you ever considered how much of your life you live in fear? Much of my life has been robbed of peace because of it. Simply put, it is impossible for fear and peace to coexist.

But the joy-killer of fear doesn't hold a candle to the destructive final step of this dastardly three-step dance. The end result is what kills the masculine soul: "So I hid." Little boys play hide-and-seek, but when Adam hid from God, he embraced spiritual death. He no longer experienced the abundant life of intimacy with Father God. He was plucked out of the safe and fulfilling place of community—both with God and his lifelong mate, Eve.

Isolated Nightmare

When Adam hid from God because of shame about his sin, the first man stumbled into what would become every man's nightmare: ISOLATION. That's right. Man's primary problem is isolation, a trait that resulted from original sin. While this may come as a surprise to some of you reading these words, isolation is the overarching, daunting, disaster-sparking problem of males in the twenty-first century. Man's primary obstacles are NOT things like:

- Lust and pornography
- Lack of Bible knowledge
- Spiritual warfare
- Selfishness
- Childhood wounds
- Anger
- Addiction
- Prayerlessness

All the problems on this list are issues flowing from one, singular issue: hiding.

Isolation is our biggest issue as men. When men from different churches came together and became serious about discipling men in East Texas, we discovered an amazing truth: if a man chooses to come out of hiding and enter into intimate relationships with Christian brothers, he is transformed. He becomes spiritually healthy, deeply connected to Father God, and finds freedom over habitual sins. In essence, he comes alive.

This truth was shocking to me. I had been an ordained minister for almost twenty years, but had no idea that simply destroying isolation in men's lives would be totally life-changing.

Take men like Michael, who came into our brotherhood several years ago after struggling with pornography daily for twenty-five years. He was married to a godly woman and had a beautiful daughter. On three different occasions, Michael reached out to spiritual leaders in an effort to get help, but each time was faced a letdown.

In desperation, he attended one of our men's bootcamps. The look on his face wordlessly proclaimed his story—nearly consumed by despair, he was on the verge of giving up. On the first night of bootcamp, Michael had the opportunity to bring his pornographic darkness into the marvelous light. He crucified his pride and confessed everything about his ugly porn habit. Two compassionate men sat with him and lovingly received every ounce of his confession. These two brothers offered no judgements, no answers, and no battle plans. They just showered this humble man with the explosive love of Jesus.

Michael came out of hiding that night. When he did, God set him free. His primary problem was not the sin of lust and porn--it was isolation. The pain of hiding in solitary confinement of his daily struggles had kept him trapped in sexual bondage. The fact he found freedom illustrates how God created man solely for relationship. It's the bottom line of our existence. Whether we realize it or not, we crave intimacy with God and others in every moment of our lives. We cannot escape this yearning for community.

Adam died spiritually when he chose to disobey God and then hide from Him. This resulted in replacing relationship with isolation. At this point, Adam lost everything that meant anything. He went bankrupt in the worst possible way.

Fully Restored

You know the rest of the story. God was keenly aware of man's plight and solved the dilemma in the most perfect way possible by sending His Son, Jesus, to die for us. In doing so, Jesus took every ounce of sin and every shred of shame that you and I would ever experience. Jesus endured this torture for one reason: so that men (and women) could once again live fully naked and unashamed.

He fully restored the nudist colony! Well, not really—at least not like the Ponderosa Ranch. Christ died so that every one of us could live a naked and unashamed lifestyle. Jesus Christ is doing only one thing right now: restoring relational intimacy with God and others. Miraculously. Everywhere. Every human being on the planet craves this intimacy. This was the purpose of the cross: to destroy isolation once and for all for anyone who receives the free gift of eternal life in Christ.

It is a profound privilege to know each other deeply and to be deeply known by others. There is no other way to stay spiritually alive without transparent, honest, intimate relationships. The Bible calls this "church." My friend, Michael, calls it true freedom.

Yet, in American church culture (whether in the South, the Midwest, or the Northeast), Christian men face a profound dilemma. Many good-hearted, godly men have gone back into hiding. They have not given up on Jesus; some serve as deacons, elders, and mighty servants of God. I wouldn't question their spiritual commitment. Many of them read the Bible daily and rarely miss a church service. Yet, because they have been duped just like Adam, they have reaped the same results of fear and hiding.

I believe the majority of church-going men live a painful, defeated life of isolation. However, the greater tragedy derives from the fact that nobody knows they are sad and defeated because the first thing we do in hiding is pull on a mask. Just as Adam grabbed the nearest fig leaf to cover himself for fear of exposure, so do many Christian men. If we are honest, we are all tempted daily to display our favorite mask and hide our true hearts from others-- I know that I am.

Wearing a Mask

Not too long ago I had a long talk with a brother named Tim. He asked how my heart was doing. I was quick to tell him about a breakthrough with my daughter, but withheld the truth about a painful struggle with my finances. Embarrassed to reveal the truth, I put on a mask. I knew better, but I did it anyway. When I hid, I missed an opportunity to be naked and unashamed. I rejected the gift of God loving me through the ministry of a trusted friend, and Tim missed out on the opportunity to be used by God to minister to me. So, we both lost, all because I chose to hide.

As one of the leaders of the East Texas men's movement, I can quickly put on the "Men's Pastor" mask. There I can hide and pretend that all is well with my soul. I can share passionately about what God is doing in the lives of men all around me. I can pretend that my heart is overwhelmed with joy because I have the privilege of watching men be transformed. But on many occasions, I have no joy. The pain only intensifies when I put on a mask and then I topple back into the despair of isolation. The monster of shame has me in his clutches.

As always, this shame produces fear. I am afraid that I will not be accepted if I am honest about my doubts and struggles.

So, I often go through my day meeting with people with my mask intact. I can remain there for several hours, or even days at a time, suffering silently as I pretend that all is well with my soul. I can deceive myself so easily. I can point to the positive circumstances of my life, the blessings of God, and maybe even the fruit of my ministry. I can tell myself, "Life is good, and my heart is healthy." But it is not. I am isolated. I am wearing a mask.

And then it happens. I find myself sitting face-to-face with a good, godly brother, and what my soul is screaming for is now right in front of me. I want freedom. I crave intimacy. I am tired of this ridiculous mask! I look into the eyes of the man in front of me as my heart silently cries, "Please help me crawl out of the cave of isolation."

I take a deep breath and open my mouth. I quickly find my masculine, God-given voice and honestly confess. I declare my pain, my sin, my struggles. I humbly share the one thing that I don't want anybody to know. When I do, I step out of the death-grip of isolation and into the marvelous light of Christ that is found when I am intimately known by others. Once again, I am free.

You can be too. I will show you how. Welcome to the brotherhood.

CHAPTER 3

Invitation of a Lifetime

I have good news for you: men's ministry doesn't work. At least not for 99 percent of the churches in America. In recent years, I have talked to many burnt-out, frustrated men's ministry leaders who are taking a lengthy sabbatical from their duties. Each of these godly, capable leaders has the exact same story, revolving around the same three-phase cycle:

Phase I: The Launch Phase: Excitement time! Something new is about to launch. Maybe it is the latest and greatest men's book, complete with cool videos, perfect for a twelve-week study. It could be a weekend retreat with skeet shooting and a wild game feast. A father-son banquet or a daddy-daughter dance. This phase is full of vision and passion, brimming with hopes and dreams.

Phase II: The Maintenance Phase: The goal here is to keep the programs going: the weekly accountability groups, monthly prayer breakfasts, or the Bible study in Ephesians. This phase is marked by more hard work and less enthusiasm.

Phase III: The Termination Phase: At this point, men's ministry has morphed into a burden for the leadership team. Attendance has dwindled and frustration has set in. Big time. "Thank goodness summer is here; let's take a break until fall!"

This perpetual cycle can occur repeatedly during the life of a congregation. All that is required is a new batch of men's leaders with fresh passion and a new program, sprinkled with several new members eager to learn. Yet I wonder how many church leaders pause to ask the obvious question: Why doesn't our men's ministry work?

The answer is simple. In fact, you likely already know the answer. The traditional men's ministry doesn't work and never will, for one basic reason: It is too easy to hide. Let's face it. Many discipleship programs become fig leaves to cover up what is really going on inside the hearts of the men. They don't intend to do this, but it inevitably happens. Look at the "top ten" list for men's ministry opportunities:

1. Annual men's retreat
2. Accountability groups
3. Saturday morning prayer breakfast
4. "Beast Feast"
5. Men's Bible study
6. Dove hunt/fishing trip
7. Men's or father-son campout
8. Workday at the church
9. Men's conference
10. Outreach to the community

All of the above are good activities, with real potential to impact men. The problem is they all share the same weakness: no invitation to be real and experience the true power of brotherhood. The focal point is either learning, doing, or fellowshipping. The truth about learning, doing, and fellowshipping is that a man can successfully carry out all three of these activities and still be painfully isolated in his journey with Christ.

Before going any further, I want to be clear about how I feel concerning the local church: passionate. I believe wholeheartedly, without reservation, in God's eternal, Christ-ordained, one-and-only vehicle for His Kingdom—the local church. I spent almost a decade of my life in full-time pastoral ministry and will do anything to help any church fulfill its vision. Like other grassroots movements in other areas of the nation, the men's discipleship movement in East Texas exists ONLY to serve pastors and empower the ministry of the local church. I love the church and all its pastors.

Destructiveness of Hiding

That said, I also refuse to live in denial concerning the weakness of the church in discipling the hearts of men. Even rock-solid, Bible-teaching churches struggle when it comes to destroying isolation in the lives of men. Until the masks come off, discipling men is exceedingly difficult.

I think of Jason, who was passionate about his weekly men's Bible study every Thursday morning at 6:30. He enjoyed the verse-by-verse approach and the spirited discussions. Unfortunately he was also developing a passion for witty, attractive, shapely Sue, his new assistant at work.

Jason was confident that he could keep things under control. After all, he still cared for his beautiful wife of twelve years. Unfortunately, Jason underestimated the power of keeping things in the dark because of his ignorance about the destructive power of hiding. He was afflicted with man's primary problem: isolation.

It was only a matter of time before the darkness swallowed him whole. Unable to confide in a brother about his struggles and temptations, Jason gradually—step by step, seductive glance by seductive glance, innocent joke by playful remark—fell into a sexual relationship with his assistant. Six months later, Jason's precious wife found out about the affair. He literally lost everything that mattered.

I still wonder how the story would have turned out if Jason had an authentic brotherhood? What if his Thursday morning group had been committed to total honesty and zero mask-wearing? What if he had just two spiritual friends whom he trusted completely? What if Jason would have run to these brothers the first day he felt an attraction to Sue? I am convinced there would have been a radically different outcome.

Do you remember the first two sentences of this chapter? Feel free to turn back the page and read them again. The truth that men's ministry doesn't work truly is good news. In fact, it is excellent news!

How can this be?

Believe it or not, men in the church are hungering and thirsting for something that *does work.* Men will not fully engage in the life of the church until we give them something different. Their souls are starving for something more life-giving than a new men's Bible study, a cookout, a deacons meeting, or a mission trip. They may not get too excited about listening to an energetic, enthusiastic speaker at the next pancake breakfast, either.

Before passing off men as largely chauvinistic, pleasure-seeking slugs, recognize that a man's lack of commitment has nothing to do with his spiritual health. These men are not being stubborn, prideful, or selfish. They are spiritually hungry, desperate for something authentic and powerful. A man's lack of commitment in the church is a cry for more. It is a voice declaring: *"Give me something that will make me come alive!"*

The men in your church are screaming for something that will wake up their masculine souls in the midst of a feminist-saturated society that often seeks to obliterate their very nature or at least consign it to irrelevance. They probably do not know exactly what that looks like; they just know when they are not getting it.

Ministry Failure

While it is good news that men's ministry doesn't work, the even better news is that something *does.* Namely, the biblical alternative:

just do what Jesus did. I had to learn this the hard way. I spent almost a decade of my life as a full-time pastor in a wonderful church, yet all the time was spent doing ministry much differently than Jesus.

Now, from the outside looking in, people thought that we were on the cutting edge of building the Kingdom of God in our region. Many applauded our efforts. As one of the fastest-growing churches in town, in five years we mushroomed from a congregation of 90 to 750. With nearly two dozen weekly home groups to disciple and pastor, you could sense the excitement as soon as you walked in the doors on any given Sunday morning.

Yet for the most part, we failed. The vast majority of our members lived in isolation (even regular attendees at our small groups). Very few had a lifestyle of relationally making disciples. Caught up in the church growth frenzy of the 1990's, driven by several noted megachurches, I failed to recognize that the American model of ministry IS NOT conducive to making disciples. Pastors typically devote the bulk of their time to the typical job description of keeping the machine humming.

As I came to grips with the superficial nature of my ministry and its failure to help people grow spiritually, I lost my excitement about the Sunday morning machine. Reflecting during this painful period, I had to confess that much of my ministry had been about me and my ego. Finally, I made the decision to peacefully step aside from my paid pastoral position.

After leaving the church, I spent the next three months wrestling with God and having my heart purified. Repenting of pastoral pride was excruciating.

Eventually, I arose from the ashes, filled with more passion for ministry than ever. Only now I burned with desperation over how to make fully devoted followers of Christ. I will never forget the day I made this pledge: *"I will learn how to relationally disciple the hearts of men, just like Jesus did, no matter the cost."*

In April of 1999, I grabbed a few good buddies, said goodbye to my contemporary ministry methods, and embraced the Jesus model of relational discipleship. It wasn't easy. I had received a lot of strokes from pastoral ministry as I taught, counseled, led, and administrated. Naturally, it was a slow, tenuous start for all of us. But we learned, and as we did, it turned our world upside down. Indeed, we were shocked at the huge amount of lasting spiritual fruit we witnessed in men's lives.

Once we did, we realized there would be no turning back. What Jesus did two thousand years ago worked perfectly, and it still does. There is no need to create something new, relevant, or innovative to draw in busy men. Just do what Jesus did and you will find it impossible to go wrong.

Strategic DNA

So exactly what did Jesus do? He built an authentic brotherhood. Slowly. One man at a time. This was the essence of Christ's three-year ministry on the earth. He assembled a small band of brothers; twelve ordinary, flawed, weak men. Men just like you and me. But this small group was not the kind you will find in most churches. These guys did not come together to discuss a passage of Scripture, create the annual church budget, or conduct deacon business. Although ordinary in appearance, these guys were more like a squad of Navy SEALs.

The DNA of this group consisted of the very elements that make every man come fully alive. There would be no need to preach to these guys about commitment because these men were sold out to the cause. They found what they had been looking for their entire lives. The opportunity that Jesus presented sparked their healthy masculine desires. They were created for this!

So how are Christian men created? We must fiercely wrestle with this question if the church hopes to seriously fulfill its call to disciple men. There are three key, basic elements our men's ministry believe that make a Christian man come alive. Since they will bring out the best in a man every time, they must be the DNA of any strategic initiative to disciple men. I will use the acronym PAL to describe it:

Purpose
Adventure
Love

Let me be clear from the outset. It doesn't matter how you make this happen, because there are a thousand ways to do it. You can use our unique strategy or make up your own. Just make sure that you have genuine love, a ton of adventure, and a huge Kingdom purpose.

Finding Purpose

Let's start with the first element: PURPOSE. Most men are bored in church for one overriding reason: they don't have a Kingdom purpose. While they don't mind serving as an usher, deacon, or parking lot attendant, it doesn't tap into their longing for eternal significance. Every man has an inborn desire to be a part of something larger than himself. We all want our lives to make a difference in the world.

Why? It's the Christ in us. God created men as world changers. We are aware at some level that the "Christ in us" can bring transformation to a sinful world. Most men just don't know how. The brotherhood, building at the grassroots level in East Texas, is waking men up to this reality. In our town, I am watching men walk shoulder-to-shoulder for the primary purpose of changing the world one man at a time.

Not too long ago, I received a call from Dan. He was so excited, I thought he was going to hyperventilate on the phone. He was leaving his men's meeting and felt overwhelmed by what God did.

A new guy named Bart had miraculously found their group and stumbled in, thinking it was a Bible study. Instead, he discovered it was a group of men, being gut-level honest. Opening his heart, Bart and the men encountered God together. After chatting for a while, the leader asked Bart if he wanted to say anything. Feeling accepted, Bart confessed that his wife had just told him she wanted a divorce. Next, with a group of men he had just met, Bart poured out his pain amid gushing tears.

In that moment, God reminded Dan and his brothers of their purpose: to change the world, one man at a time. In the coming days, Bart will experience the power and redemption of Christ because of this band of brothers. The world will be changed because another man was transformed by the revolution Jesus began.

Yearning for Adventure

The second element is ADVENTURE. It's built into the heart of every man. My son, Austin, is the perfect example. His hobby is jumping off objects such as 4,000 ft. cliffs in Brazil, the Perrine Bridge in Idaho, and an occasional radio antenna. He is a skydiver and base jumper and will only get into a plane if allowed to jump out at 14,000 feet! In late 2020, two months after finishing two years of active duty with the National Guard, my son began a new career as a tandem skydiving instructor. He currently makes his living jumping out of planes with people strapped to his chest. It seems his masculine soul can't get too much adventure!

Having the element of adventure in your men's discipleship means one thing: aside from Sunday morning worship, you won't be able to do much with your men in the church building. Even deer mounts hanging in the lobby won't make for an adventurous setting for a man. But your pastor won't mind men hanging out elsewhere because when he sees men come alive in Christ; in fact, the pastor will be more excited than anyone else. I have never seen a pastor who wasn't thrilled watching men get set free from habitual sins, love their wives and kids deeply, and start reaching out to other men.

So why is adventure so crucial in discipling men? Because it always involves a challenge, which is what men want. The only question is whether the church will give men a spiritual challenge or allow them to waste their lives on the challenges the world provides. Can you imagine the challenges the twelve disciples faced during their three years with Jesus? Hardship. Persecution. People with impossible needs. No idea where their next meal was coming from. Their masculine souls loved every minute of it.

That's because men love risk. It's the bare essence of faith. Men were created to take huge risks; our faith is not real without it. It's what makes men come alive. To live a comfortable, secure life is to live no life. Hence, why most men's ministries don't last long. Men would rather go to the golf course and take the risk of hitting the green in two shots on a par five hole than sit through another Bible study.

Are you willing to give the men in your church a spiritual adventure that will force them out of their comfort zone? If so, you will empower men to experience an important ingredient to manhood: passion. It's part of our adventurous spirits. Passion is the expression of a man fully alive. Living passionately means truly embracing the challenges of life, having courage to drink deeply of the pain, and jumping off the cliff of comfort into the embrace of God. Adventure leads to passion, and a church without passionate men is dead.

Men can no longer sit in a safe circle, Bible in hands, and discuss the miracles and excitement of the book of Acts. We must experience it! We must lead men into the dangerous land of following Christ and setting the captives free. Every man in your church was created for this adventure. We have learned that if you give a man a God-sized challenge, he will rise to the occasion and be the man that God created him to be.

Our primary spiritual adventure is called "Men's Bootcamp." It's a huge challenge for every man that signs up. Most men say they would not have gone if they knew what they were signing up for. Every man hits a breaking point at some time during the weekend. Every man pushes through by simply trusting God and letting other men help him. Only the church can provide the adventure that men crave. And the time has come for the church to do this very thing.

Craving Affirmation

Finally, there is the element of LOVE. Men are funny when it comes to our desperate need to be loved. We don't talk about this craving to be accepted and affirmed by other men, and yet our hearts are starving for it. The only way that a band of brothers will survive past the one-year mark is that each man feels deeply cared for and accepted. Every man in your church (especially the pastor) hungers for unconditional love. It's how we are wired.

When it comes to this kind of love, you can't fool a man. I am talking about pure, unconditional love. The kind that declares, "I care deeply about your soul regardless of what you do or don't do." If there is a hidden agenda for connecting with a guy, like adding his name to the church roll, finding a new youth group leader, or enlisting him in church workdays, he will sniff it out.

I get phone calls or texts quite often from a man named Todd. He is always quick to remind me of who I am in Christ. I have no doubt concerning this man's love and commitment for me. He says these words out loud with authenticity, power, and authority: "I love you, Brian Childres." When it comes to helping me be the best man I can be, he holds nothing back. I can literally call this brother any time of day or night, about anything.

One might expect this kind of love would be a no-brainer for the church. Scripture makes it clear that without love, we are nothing. Love is the catalyst of discipling men. Yet, you and

I both know the painful truth—many good-hearted Christians, including myself, would rather study and talk about sacrificial love than experience the inconvenience and pain of practicing it. I can promise one thing, though. If you model how to care for the souls of men with the fierce love of Christ, you will experience a revival in your church.

Visions of Power

Are you getting a vision of what can happen with the men that God has placed in your life? The men sitting in the pews of every church in America are hungry to be a part of this movement, whether they know it or not. When I share the PAL vision with a pastor or a men's ministry leader, there is usually a flicker of hope; they get a glimpse of a new way of leading and discipling men. Then comes the big question: "What will it take for this vision to become a reality in our church?"

The answer is simple: just two men. That's all. Just you and one of your friends. Remember, we're talking about a *relational* disciple-making movement, NOT a ministry. So, it can easily start with one relationship between two ordinary men. These two men don't need a ton of talent or knowledge, just a love for God and others.

For me, it took a while to develop this kind of close discipleship. Finally, in the summer of 2008, we got serious and shifted into high gear. That summer I hopped into a Ford F-250 pickup driven by my buddy, Paul Roberts, and headed for a suburb of Nashville, Tennessee. We spent that weekend with a group of men who were serious about the brotherhood of Jesus Christ. They were living it with such passion that we heard about their powerful testimonies from six hundred miles away. We hungered to see the same kind of authentic relationships closer to home.

What we witnessed on that visit was the most powerful display of godly love between men that we had ever seen. Their vulnerability and transparency gave birth to a power that I desperately wanted for my own life and friendships. These men created a safe place for me to deeply mourn and weep for the long-buried sins in my life. Their commitment to me, a man they were meeting for the first time, was life changing.

Paul and I left Tennessee with a crystal-clear calling: to do just what the guys in the Nashville area were doing—to do whatever it takes to destroy isolation, one man at a time, and watch God build a brotherhood that would change East Texas and the world. We said, "Yes" to that call. Since that day, we have made a lot of mistakes, and yet God has built a powerful and ever-growing band of brothers in our region. This movement of transformed men has resulted in restored marriages, encouraged pastors, and stronger local churches.

The miracles have only just begun. God is multiplying this movement in several other states and regions, most of them I won't know about until I get to heaven. The Holy Spirit is like that, working quietly in ways that don't attract headlines or make the evening news, and yet in ways that change the world. So, I extend the invitation to you, my friend. If you are hungry to be a part of this journey, let's take the next step.

CHAPTER 4

Rites of Initiation

Initiation is a lost art in our modern culture. We don't initiate our men like they do in other places in the world. Take Brazil, for example, where deep in the heart of the Amazon jungle lives an indigenous tribe of more than thirteen thousand called the Satere-Mawe. To become a man in this tribe, a boy must stick his hand in a glove woven with bullet ants and withstand the stings for ten minutes without uttering a sound.

According to the Schmidt Pain Index, the bullet ant has the worst sting in the ant world. The sting continues for twenty-four hours, and is described as carrying throbbing, all-consuming pain. The tribesmen make the glove by knocking out the bullet ants with a natural sedative. While the killer ants are asleep, the elders weave them into a glove made of leaves with the ant's stingers facing inwards.

When the ants arise from their slumber, the excitement begins. The boy puts on the glove and endures pure hell. The amount of venom he receives causes his arm to be paralyzed temporarily and leaves him shaking uncontrollably for days.

How's that for an initiation? The East Texas brotherhood is a big fan of initiation also. We just happen to carry it out a bit differently than the Satere-Mawe! Yet such rites are a vital part of moving from isolation to intimacy. It is easy to have friends. Spiritual effort and time is required if a man wants real brothers.

Removing Masks

So how does a grown man get initiated into the brotherhood of Jesus? In essence, it is stripping a man of all masks. Removing all fig leaves. To destroy isolation, one must completely come out of hiding. A man must bring all things out of the dark and into the light of Christ. While this is uncomfortable, it also provides the freedom that we crave.

But why must a man be stripped of his masks to be a part of the brotherhood? Why can't a guy just sign up and attend weekly meetings? Because initiation is what separates authentic brotherhood from just another small group, one that may nibble around the edges of camaraderie, but never dives deep. To be real brothers, there must be real love. And before you can love the real me, you must know the real me.

Listen to what pastor and speaker John Lynch has to say about relating while keeping our masks intact, "No one told me that when I wear a mask, only my mask receives love. We can gain admiration and respect from behind a mask. We can even intimidate. But as long as we're behind a mask, any mask, we will not be able to receive love. Then, in our desperation to be loved, we'll run to fashion more masks, hoping the next will give us what we're longing for: to be known, accepted, trusted, and loved."[1]

It is impossible to be brothers until we remove all the masks. Keep faking it and all you get is empty religion. Religion is when one spiritual mask relates to another spiritual mask. Jesus hated religion. Most men do, too. There is only one way to join Jesus in His men's movement: a man must be stripped of the poser while committing to help other men do the same. We join the revolution only when we become naked and unashamed.

So how does being stripped of our masks produce this awesome band of brothers? The secret sauce to the whole thing is found in 2 Corinthians 12:9-10:

My grace is sufficient for you, for my power is made perfect in weakness. Therefore, I will boast all the more gladly about my weaknesses, so that Christ's power may rest on me. That is why, for Christ's sake, I delight in weaknesses, in insults, in hardships, in persecutions, in difficulties. For when I am weak, then I am strong.

This is an insane truth. Read it one more time as you let it sink deeply into your heart. This revelation can be difficult to spiritually digest; it can take many years before a man fully embraces this passage. Some never do. Yet these two verses contain the secret to true masculine power. When men finally quit pretending, they discover their most prized possession as men: *weakness.*

At first this is shocking. Many men have spent the entirety of their lives running from their weakness. They despise their frailty and have connected weakness with being wimpy.

Because of their fear and hatred of their weaknesses, they have hidden their sins and struggles from everyone, resulting in painful isolation. Thus, the greatest epidemic among Christian men is despising our weakness.

Stepping into Community

The opposition to weakness changes when a man takes his first small step into community with other weak men. True initiation reveals the liberating truth of a man's weakness: *When we are weak, then we are strong.* This revelation transforms everything. When a man begins to feel at home in his weakness, he has no desire to go back to being a poser. He may become as radical as the apostle Paul and actually boast about his frailty. When was the last time you threw a party for your sexual temptations? Weakness is not despised in God's community of men. Rather, it is prized and celebrated. Whether we believe it or not, in our weakness Christ's strength is perfected.

The powerhouse effect of weakness causes a man to see his need for God. Our need for God always results in our need for one another. In essence, it is our weakness as men that gives birth to a powerful brotherhood. A brand-new small group ministry for men is not the same as a healthy army of men in your church. The brotherhood of Jesus Christ only exists where weak men acknowledge the truth. When was the last time that you, in your God-given weakness, cried out for help to another man?

I called Ted recently to discuss an upcoming Men's Bootcamp. We chatted for five minutes; as we were ending the call he said, "Hey, I need to tell you something. I looked at an image online this morning that I shouldn't have. I know that if I don't bring it into the light right now, I will be tempted to take the next step by looking at porn, and then to masturbate. So, I'm confessing it to you."

I was honored, humbled, and inspired by his vulnerability. Ted is a man who knows the power of his weakness. He is convinced that declaring his neediness is the key to real power. I want to live my life like this man. Over the past decade we have seen hundreds of men come alive in Christ simply because they demonstrated courage and acknowledged their weakness. This is always the catalyst for revival. Once a man humbles himself, the heavens open and miracles take place. My privilege as a men's disciple-maker is to lead a man into this place of humility.

What happens once a man is convinced that he is needy? The initiation begins! For some men, this process takes just a few days. For others, it may take several months. Some linger for years. But the time factor is irrelevant. What matters is that a man gets intimately connected to the brotherhood. It's what Paul meant when he talked about being a member of the body of Christ. In essence, it's Church Membership Class 101.

The Five Steps

Here is a practical overview of the five steps that most men take when going through the empowering process of initiation. Remember, there is no right way to lead a man through this rite. Believe me, you will know when initiation has happened. The exciting transformation contained in the Bible will begin to happen in your men's movement.

The first step is CONFESSION of any unconfessed sins. We have discovered that every man has at least one deep, dark secret. It is a difficult endeavor to live in total freedom when we hide things in the closet of our souls. Darkness destroys while light gives life. James 5:16 offers every man an iron-clad guarantee if we will humble ourselves: "Confess your sins to each other and pray for each other so that you may be healed."

One of my favorite declarations to hear from a new brother is "That is the first time I have ever told that to anyone in my entire life!" Confession is the ultimate in spiritual relief.

The next step is confessing your FEARS. This is crucial because our fears expose our unbelief. Most of our pain in life comes from unbelief. Scripture makes it clear that God's leading desire is that we trust Him. Of course, we all struggle with trusting God, daily. The first step to repenting of this unbelief is becoming aware of our fears.

The third step is taking off our MASKS. Recall those three tragic words from Genesis 3:8: "And they hid." We all hide. We all wear masks. Every man has been a fraud, a poser. But before we can take off our masks, we must be able to identify them. What are the top three masks that you wear? Can you identify with any of the following?

- "I'm Fine."
- Funny Guy.
- The "Answer Man."
- "Mr. Minister."

- "I'm in Control."
- The Victim.
- The "Family Man."
- Spiritual Expert.
- "Mr. Success."

Your Mask? _____

Hiding our real faces is killing us and hurting those whom we love. Let's take off the mask so we can breathe again.

The fourth step is exposing our WOUNDS. Let's face it, we have all been deeply hurt. Some men have been tragically wounded. Many of these guys live in daily torment because of one single past childhood event. When you give a man a safe place to reveal the gory pain of an open wound, you empower him to take the biggest step towards healing.

The fifth and final step is repenting of IDOLS. There is only one thing more damaging than the evil in our lives—the good things in our lives. Why? Because the good things can easily become our idols, be that our marriage, ministry, work, hobbies, food, or physical fitness. We are all prone to trying to get life and satisfaction out of something other than Jesus Christ. True freedom comes when we recognize our counterfeit gods and turn back to Jesus.

I dare you to lead your men into all five steps of initiation. Start by modeling what it means to be a true leader: YOU go first! You must be willing to be stripped of your own fig leaves if you want other men to do the same. If you humble yourself, others will follow your lead. Remember, you may not be able to do this quickly. Initiation may take a good chunk of time and it will not happen without pain. The discomfort of revealing the hidden parts of the soul is never fun, but it is worth it. You will be energized by the God encounter that happens for every man as he is fully initiated into the body of Christ.

Four Faces of Pride

There is a particular reason most men have run from weakness most of their life: pride. I have never met a man who didn't struggle immensely with it. Pride is the killer of the masculine soul. Without it, there would be no isolation. We would still be enjoying paradise in Adam's beautiful garden. Pride is what causes us to go to church and put on a smile when our marriage is in upheaval. Pride propels us to show up to our men's meeting and refuse to confess our porn indulgence the night before. Pride places a thick wall between us and other men, even when we are face to face in a small group meeting. Pride builds a cage, forces a man into it, locks the door, and watches him rot in loneliness. Pride is a ruthless force.

There are four ways in which pride is expressed—we call them the four faces of pride. Getting honest about pride can open your eyes to the root of some of your greatest struggles. I have watched hundreds of men be transformed by confessing the sin of pride and humbling themselves before God and others.

To outline them, pride's four faces include:

1. "Looking Good." If we are gut-level honest, we all want to look good. Every man has an image in their mind of the typical "good and powerful man." For some, this is a successful businessman. For others, it is the godly family man. For me, it was wearing the "effective minister" mask. I got duped into pulling on this mask in my twenties as I connected my value as a man to being seen as a powerful spiritual leader. I can still easily put on this mask and hide my true face.

2. The second face of pride is "Feeling Good." This one causes a man to do whatever it takes to avoid pain. He refuses to enter into the painful areas of the heart and into difficult conversations with people close to him while pretending everything is fine. I've known men whose marriage is in shambles, have credit card bills stacked higher than their monthly income, are captive to an

alcohol or drug addiction, but when someone asks them how they are, the reply is: "I'm fine." A man who refuses to embrace pain is a man who refuses to truly live.

3. The third face of pride is "Being Right." This man places his "correct" knowledge above all else. He never backs down from a debate. Indeed, he is passionate about wanting others to see and believe exactly as he does because to be wrong about anything is a discomfort that he cannot bear. Tragically, his right-fighting deeply wounds his family and those close to him. He is blind to the fact that his "being right" profits little and causes much destruction.

4. The fourth face of pride is the main instigator of all the above. It is called "Being in Control." All men wrestle with this beast as we waste considerable time attempting to control our lives. In our finite minds, we think we know what is best, so we strategize, manipulate, influence others, and expend huge amounts of time, money, and energy trying to control everything. It is our grand effort to make our lives work. How sad! The truth is that no man will ever be in control of any part of his life at any time. Thanks be to God that we don't have to be in control. God is big enough.

Causing Pain

Which of these faces of pride are causing you unnecessary pain? Simply recognizing your primary pride issue is a huge step toward destroying isolation. We must identify the monster before we can destroy him.

My friend Barry had a wake-up call many years ago concerning his ridiculous desire to "look good." Here's how he relates his story:

"I was convicted by the Holy Spirit that I was highly selective in my transparency with my brothers. My strategy was simple: confess the painless sins and hide the embarrassing ones. In reality, I was a fake. Pride had its death grip on my soul. How many times had I lied to the men who loved me deeply? How many times had I missed a God encounter because of my hiding?

"I sat down with a pen and paper. I decided to write down everything that I had been keeping in the dark. I was shocked at one of the first words that landed on the paper. I stared at the word. Had I ever uttered this word out loud as a personal confession? I knew without a doubt that I hadn't. Ever.

"What was the word staring back at me? Masturbation. I had struggled with masturbation for over twenty years and had never confessed it as a sin to anyone. Why? I had a ranking system for sin, and masturbation was one of the nasty, perverted ones! I didn't want to be seen as nasty and perverted. I wanted to look good. I wanted to look like a holy, righteous spiritual leader. I bought into the lie. The lie that says having an outer form of holiness is appealing. But it's not. It is appalling.

"After I completed the list, I immediately called my friend Bill. I asked him for one hour of his time. I told him all that he had to do was show up, look me in the eyes, and listen to me dump my guts. We met at 6:30 a.m. the next Thursday. I went straight for the jugular vein of my pride with no hesitation. 'I struggle with masturbation,' I said. What a relief. Darkness was thrown into the light.

"My most painful confession was with Jerry. I met with him the following week. Jerry was a younger man who I had discipled for over a decade. The tragedy was that Jerry had struggled with masturbation for many years. Unfortunately, previously I had implied that I did not. What a deceived Pharisee I had been in my relationship with him.

"We met on a Friday morning. I felt sick to my stomach as I prepared to come clean. I wept as I confessed my sin of deception and asked his forgiveness. He received my repentance with much gratitude."

Barry finally got to a point in his life where he refused to let pride continue to devour him. A man must get desperate in order to kick pride in the teeth.

A Rude Awakening

As for me, I was convinced that I had been fully initiated into the brotherhood. After all, I had been the chief creator of our bootcamp and had been living this stuff for several years. Little did I know, I was about to experience an initiation like none other.

It happened in 2011, which I saw as the best year of my life. When summertime came, I was riding high. I had just finished officiating a wedding for a Grammy-Award-winning musical artist in front of a multitude of music and movie stars. The bride and groom tried their best to hide the wedding venue from the media. I happened to be standing alone with the groom outside, waiting for the ceremony to begin. Then, in a split second, a paparazzi helicopter exploded into view and proceeded to snap a few pictures of us. What an adrenaline rush! A truly wild and memorable day!

My wife and I returned from this adventure to a ministry that was beginning to explode. Our Men's Boot Camps had transformed many men and churches, with leaders getting excited about setting men free and building a powerful brotherhood. In addition, the business I had established after leaving full-time pastoral ministry was thriving. It provided a six-figure income and allowed me the flexibility to pour a ton of time into the men's movement while enjoying quality time with my family.

That July, my wife and our two children had the best two-week vacation of our lives, cruising up and down the Pacific Northwest coastline. Needless to say, abundant blessings came my way during the first nine months of 2011. It was truly the best of times. Or so I thought. Then came Tuesday, October 11th at approximately 8:45 a.m. It came in the form of an email I opened just after reaching the office: my wife was leaving me.

In an instant, I fell from the top of my mountain into a valley of devastation. I had no idea such horrific pain even existed. Even today, I have no words to describe the level of torment and despair that haunted me during those days. I wasn't just gut-punched, I was stripped naked. Totally exposed and my idol of the perfect marriage revealed as a sham.

In the days and weeks that followed, my masks melted off my face, leaving a huge, gaping, bleeding wound-- one the whole world could see. I could not teach, serve, minister, or lead. I could do absolutely nothing, except be me. The real me. All my fears, sins, wounds, idols, and masks were flushed out into the light. No more hiding. No more pretending to be Mr. All-Star Minister.

Thankfully, the pain did not destroy my soul. My brothers would not let that happen. They came to my rescue literally every day as I climbed an excruciating mountain ordained by God himself. As I look back now, the destruction of my marriage became my true initiation into the brotherhood. In all my time on the planet, I had never been more desperately needy. Overnight I went from being a successful men's ministry leader to being a desperately needy member of the brotherhood.

It was, without a doubt, the most powerful season of my life. Why? I was fully initiated into a band of brothers who will stick with me until I die. I have no doubts about their love for me because I know these weak brothers will lay down their lives for me if need be. I wish there was a way to experience the power of brotherhood without going through the pain of initiation. Yet, like all of life, if we earnestly desire joy, we must embrace the pain.

There are no shortcuts to building a tried-and-true band of brothers. Each man must be fully initiated. The good news is that every man hungers to experience the acceptance and grace that comes from initiation. It's how we were created. No man enjoys living his life while wearing a mask. Every man is screaming for help to remove it. Will you help the men in your church take off the mask?

CHAPTER 5

Priority of the Heart

It's been a few years, but I'll never forget my first sonogram. It was a weird experience feeling my nerves jump as the technician placed the cold, greasy lotion on my skin and then pressed down the transmitter. The good news: I'm not pregnant!

Well, I really did get a sonogram, but it was on my neck. They were checking to see if those two big arteries running from my heart to my brain were clean or clogged and help doctors determine if I was a stroke candidate. It was one of seven tests I had done at the local hospital. They were running a steal of a deal all for just $149. Stress tests, EKG, and other kinds of cardiovascular excitement. What a bargain!

Since I'm barely in the middle-age category, I'm not too fearful of having a cardiac event at this point in my life. While the twenty-somethings wouldn't agree, I see myself as a young buck. I can keep up with college-aged guys when we backpack up and down the mountains in nearby Arkansas. I am asking God to give me several more decades before I crash heaven's gates.

However, of this much I am certain—my body is totally dependent on the *heart*. I know that I must take care of my heart. The same is true when it comes to the privilege of loving God and others. It boils down to the same thing: our spiritual heart is the only thing that matters. Proverbs 4:23 makes a bold statement: "Above all else, guard your heart, for everything you do flows from it."

This is a profound truth. Every action that we take, every word we speak, and every attempt we make to love others flows from deep within. Author and ministry leader, John Eldredge, had this to say about the centrality of the heart in his bestseller, *Wild at Heart*: "For above all else, the Christian life is a love affair of the heart. It cannot be lived primarily as a set of principles or ethics. It cannot be managed with steps and programs. The truth of the gospel is intended to free us to love God and others with our whole heart."[1]

Heart Condition

Given these realities, I need to ask you the all-important question: How is your heart today? A sick heart will destroy a man. Guaranteed. It may take months or decades, but it will happen. We can place the blame on anger, lust, alcoholism, workaholism, or relationship failures, but the real culprit is always a sick heart.

I wrote this chapter while on a one-month sabbatical in southwest Colorado. My cabin, warmed only when I remembered to add wood to the stove, was in the middle of nowhere. One Sunday I decided to make the forty-five minute drive into town. Randomly choosing a church, I arrived just as worship began.

As soon as the last song came to an end, the pastor took the stage. Visibly shaken, he had barely started to speak when he began to cry. I quickly realized that I had shown up on a very non-typical Sunday. This broken minister withheld no tears as he announced the resignation of their long-time worship pastor.

While reluctant to share any details, it was clear that many in the congregation knew of the moral failure that had occurred in this man's life. I felt stunned and sick to my stomach at the thought of another good man falling. I wondered how long this church leader's heart had been sick.

I have ministered in the same community for about three decades. During that time, I have watched many godly men fall. I have seen how a neglected heart can destroy even the most spiritual man in town. There is no one who is immune from spiritual heart disease. It can attack any man at any time, regardless of how spiritually mature he may be. Am I saying that any man can be deceived? Yes. Is it true that a man can think he is following Christ, yet be inches from stepping off a cliff? Yes, again.

However, this only occurs if you live in isolation. Deception flourishes in darkness. Most men who get taken out are those attempting to follow Jesus alone, in their human strength. A sick spiritual heart is always an isolated heart. The apostle James outlines the process that a man must go through in order to experience spiritual suicide. Killing your heart involves a four-step journey as outlined in James 1:14–15:

Step 1: Desire occurs.
Step 2: Desire turns into temptation.
Step 3: Temptation gives birth to sin.
Step 4: Sin, when fully grown, leads to death.

This entire process must happen for a man to slip into trouble. James compares the journey towards sin to the birth and maturity of a human; the key point being that it doesn't happen quickly. It is *always* a process. This is good news because we know that it is impossible to get ambushed by sin. Since evil never sneaks up on a man, we will always have plenty of time to avoid making a very stupid decision.

This is where the brotherhood shines the brightest. It is very difficult to reach step four when we are consistently confessing our weakness and temptations to our brothers. Remember, temptation is not sin, but rather a holy, daily occurrence. How can I call temptation 'holy'? Because Jesus faced it every day of His life. Temptation is built into our humanity, whether we like it or not.

Benefits of Brotherhood

After extensive experience in ministry, I've realized there are two types of Christian men: 1) Those who are tempted much, and sin much because they are in isolation, 2) those who are tempted much, but sin little because they live with the protection of the brotherhood. In which group do you want to be? In which group do you want every man in your church to be?

God has given us a profound promise when it comes to avoiding sin. He guarantees in 1 Corinthians 10:13 that He will provide a way of escape for every temptation. That's a huge promise, one that shows there is divine provision to save you from the snare of sin. In practical terms, how does this safety net work? Through brothers. If you have a brotherhood, you have a very sturdy and effective trapdoor to bail you out of every sin imaginable.

All that is needed is to pick up your cell phone, call a brother (or two), and confess your unhealthy desires. This is the power of flushing darkness into the light. The principle is simple and yet profound: darkness cannot exist in the presence of light. We watch this happen every time we walk into a dark room and flip on the light switch.

How often do we flip the switch on amid the darkness that sneaks into our hearts? All it takes is one brother to come to our rescue. It is not difficult. Many men believe the lie that sin is easy and righteous living is hard. This is a ridiculous lie. In a redeemed man—a follower of the Lord Jesus—our masculine hearts crave righteousness. We have a natural inclination towards holiness because of who we are with Christ living in us.

We only get into trouble when we hide and attempt to follow Jesus in solitude, with no one close by to hear our concerns and steady our hands. Victory over sin is easily possible when you have men committed to the issues of your heart. This is why I am passionate about the brotherhood. My heart is always out in the open. I have brothers who love me enough to ask the hard questions day after day. Living my life naked and unashamed offers profound protection from deception.

When a man renounces pride, strips off all of his masks, and is initiated into the brotherhood, the result is the same every time: the heart is exposed. Once the heart is exposed, true ministry can begin.

Necessity of Relationships

I didn't understand this back when I was a pastor on staff at a church. I wrongly assumed that if I preached the authentic word of God, and the people in the pew weren't asleep, spiritual growth would be a natural byproduct of others hearing the truth. I thought that discipleship could happen without intimate relationships. Wrong!

My formula back then was 'man's biggest problem is ignorance.' Therefore, the solution is information. I had a Pharisee-like mentality that said as long as you have the correct theological information in your brain spiritual health will be the natural result.

When I first developed the desire to minister to others, I was just an eighteen-year-old kid. Back then I loved to listen to Chuck Swindoll—one of America's most beloved preachers—on the radio. My overarching goal in life was to preach like Chuck. Why? I thought that communicating biblical reference information was the main objective because of my misconception over man's biggest problem.

A few years later, I had a fascinating meeting with one of my mentors in ministry, Dr. Aubrey Malphurs, a distinguished professor at Dallas Theological Seminary. This school has been producing powerful preachers and spiritual leaders for decades. I was shocked by the words that came out of his mouth one afternoon. He had been writing a book on disciplemaking. The truth he declared that day went fiercely against the grain of the very institute that paid his salary. I will never forget when he leaned toward me, looked me in the eyes, and whispered: "You can't make disciples from the pulpit."

He was right. You can do a lot of good things in a sermon, but you can't make followers of Christ by preaching alone. The reason is simple: there is no relationship involved. Without a relationship, the heart stays hidden. Without brothers, my Christian experience becomes a lifestyle of lifeless Christian knowing and doing. In isolation, I trade in a heart fully alive for a boring, intellectual spirituality. Relationship reveals the heart, and a revealed heart is the first step to being an alive heart. Do you remember why Jesus Christ came to this earth? Not to give us a system of beliefs. He came "that (we) may have life and have it abundantly" (John 10:10 ESV). God wants our hearts to be fully alive.

I have a relatively new friend by the name of Nate, who went through our Men's Bootcamp several years ago. He is the typical Christian man who wanders into our men's movement: hardworking, church-going, a man of integrity. One thing that stood out about Nate was the fact that he had faithfully attended the same church every Sunday for thirty-five years.

He made a fascinating comment afterwards, "All of the biblical truths that I have heard in Bootcamp and from the brothers are not new. I have heard most of it before. So, why am I so different now?"

Great question! And the answer is basic. Nate finally made the quantum leap of moving his Christianity from his *head* to his *heart*. This is the huge jump of faith that all men must make if we are to experience the thrill of walking intimately with Jesus.

Huge Leap of Faith

My base-jumping son, Austin (who I mentioned in chapter 3) sent me a video one day after doing some relaxing base jumps over the Snake River in Idaho. He stepped off the railing of the bridge, did three backflips and tossed the chute out of his right hand. The chute deployed, he landed in the river, and the rescue boat grabbed him just in time! For him, it was a fun ten seconds of living life at full blast.

Thankfully, we don't push men off a bridge in our ministry. Nonetheless, a huge leap of faith is needed to move a man's faith from his head to his heart. I am convinced that a man will not have the courage to take this death-defying plunge without brothers. He will need a coach and some committed teammates for it to happen. He will need men praying *for* him and *over* him. He will need a squad of fellow comrades willing to do whatever it takes to expose his heart so that God can bring transformation.

If left on their own, most Christian men will not do the necessary spiritual work to deal with the issues of the heart. It is just too painful. Bob is a great example. He had plugged into every discipleship opportunity available in his church. While Bob knew something was dreadfully missing in his life, he wasn't sure what it was. After finishing yet another men's Bible study, he wasn't too excited to sign up for the next twelve-week session.

The good news was that his church had a small brotherhood. A friend named Thomas gave Bob the invitation of a lifetime. Although clueless about what this group was all about, Bob had nothing to lose. So, he said, "yes" to the invitation of initiation. The men in the group knew that until Bob exposed his heart, no spiritual growth was possible.

These men knew the secret to gain access to Bob's deep heart because they had committed to the truth found in Matthew 12:34: "For out of the abundance of the heart the mouth speaks" (ESV). We take this verse seriously. We know that the only way to lead a man's heart into the light is to empower him to speak. We call this helping a man "find his voice."

Many men have not found their masculine, God-given voice, leaving them acting like religious chatterboxes. Bob had been one of those men. While an effective communicator, most of his conversations had been shallow, discussing such safe topics as theological concepts, sports, politics, business, bragging about a hunting trip, or complaining about the weather.

Giving Voice to Reality

Given his situation, Bob's new spiritual buddies had a daunting task—helping him put a voice to the reality of his heart. So, they probed into his hidden life to discover the real Bob. In doing so, they gave Bob the courage to bring his soul into the spotlight. They did whatever it took during this process; they let him know that he was in a safe place so he could reveal the hidden issues of his heart and express them. Though it took a while to uncover the whole story, eventually, the reality of his soul came into the light. Here's what he revealed:

- The resentment he felt about his wife's affair nine years earlier
- His fears about not being able to support his family.
- His weekly porn habit
- The shame he felt about being forty pounds overweight
- His doubts concerning God's total acceptance
- Uncertainties over his purpose in life
- His feelings of failure about connecting with his teenage daughter
- His lack of passion in life

Wow! By concealing a mountain of pain in his heart, Bob also hid all of his struggles. The isolation was slowly killing him, like the proverbial "death by a thousand cuts." That is, until now, when his heart came into the light and revealed his neediness.

Suddenly, he had hope. Bob received a priceless gift. A group of men cared enough to destroy his isolation in a spirit of genuine love. They were willing to risk rejection and help tear off his masks. That group was a small fellowship of ordinary men. As I've said before, men just like you and me.

What happened to Bob? The same thing that happens to all men who humble themselves. Over the next couple of months, Bob experienced more freedom than he ever thought possible:

- Tom walked Bob through the forgiveness process concerning his wife's affair.
- Greg shared about his own struggle with viewing pornography on his smartphone.
- Sam committed to working out with Bob at the local gym twice a week to empower his weight loss goals.

The Jesus contained in that small brotherhood changed Bob's life. He will never be the same. Plus, now he is reaching out to help other men whose hearts have died from the cancer of isolation. Bob will never go back to a heartless form of Christianity because he is boldly committed to keeping his heart fully alive. He knows that this is only possible if he allows his brothers to help him with the issues of his heart.

Heart Issues

How are the hearts of the men in your church? As much as I love Sunday worship in my church, I am fully aware that I shake hands with at least one man every week whose story is similar to Bob's. That man is fighting a painful battle in his heart and, worst of all, he's often doing it alone.

Each week during worship, I try to take at least sixty seconds to slowly look around the auditorium and gaze into the eyes of men. I always ask myself the question, "How many men in this worship service are suffering from the pain of isolation?" This is a somber but crucial exercise for me because it reminds me that there are still men trapped in the painful snare of do-it-yourself Christianity. If Steve only knew that he doesn't have to battle porn all by himself. If Chris just had two brothers to empower him as he struggles with his wife's depression. If only Jerry had a small team of men to walk with him as he mourns his father's death.

It is a painful minute or two as I look throughout the congregation, but my heart doesn't just ache for the men. I feel for the wives, the sons, and the daughters. They are the ones who suffer when a man's soul is dead. If a man has unresolved issues of the heart, it is impossible for him to love and lead his family. That is why the brothers of East Texas are passionate about destroying isolation in *every* man in the church and outside of the church.

Not every man will be receptive to the idea of coming into the light, but it doesn't mean we won't extend the invitation.

After all, the health and future of Jesus's church hinges on this one thing: men with healthy hearts. What will it take for every man in your church to come out of isolation and find spiritual freedom?

CHAPTER 6

Being Brothers: Sharpening

I have always liked Larry. Not only does he tell it like it is, but he also sports some really cool tattoos. I listened, spellbound, the time he spoke during a men's meeting. Larry shared openly and from the heart about the long and winding path he had followed during his fervent search for real brothers. Judging by the reactions around the room, most of the men there could relate to his saga.

Larry told of serving fifteen years in the US Marines and loving every day of it.

"The great part was the camaraderie," this rugged guy said while numerous heads bobbed up and down. "It was great to be a part of a true brotherhood. But when I left the Marines, I lost my brothers. This impacted my entire life. I looked everywhere for genuine friendship. No matter where I went, places I looked, or people I met, I didn't succeed. Finally, I jumped into law enforcement, thinking that I would find it there. But I found nothing but politics. Then I decided to go through Men's Bootcamp, thank goodness. I left there on Sunday afternoon with the brotherhood that I had been desperately searching for, for so long."

Although he had experienced powerful camaraderie and moral support in the military, prior to Men's Bootcamp, Larry had never known about the authentic relationships that are part of God's army. We've heard it from men hundreds of times: "I had no idea this kind of brotherhood existed in the church." But it does. The good news is that you don't have to join the Marines to experience true brotherhood. But you do have to put on your combat boots, grab your M-16, and go to battle. We are in a war every day of our lives. And sometimes, it gets fierce.

Band of Brothers

A few years ago, Craig became the newest member of my band of brothers and quickly became a cherished friend. He was going through a hellish divorce; at the time, Craig was eight months into the most ferocious battle of his life. He had only seen his two daughters for a total of two hours during this entire time, trapped in a Byzantine, insane legal system that has no compassion for godly husbands fighting for their marriage and children.

Besides rarely seeing his daughters, Craig had lost access to his money and his truck. The upheaval had cost him his job, reducing him to scraping for survival; his only income came from a part-time job at a dollar store. Literally tossed into the streets, he relied on a friend who was renovating a house so he could flip the house. Craig made a makeshift home in the middle of the construction mess-- gives new meaning to "humble."

Yet, despite the chaos and living amid a mountain of pain, he considered himself the richest man on the planet. Why? Because it was the first time in his life that he had had brothers. He spent the first forty-two years of his life trying to fight his battles alone; now he had support. Brothers now reach out to him every day, sometimes just to remind him of four powerful words—the same ones that have changed the lives of so many men: "You are not alone."

I find great joy in looking a man in the eyes and reminding him that he is not alone. This one truth can deliver a man from deep discouragement. When a man's eyes are opened to the fact that he has a weapon-clad man on his left and right, another in front of him, and yet another behind him, everything changes. This is vital. Through years of coming alongside men who are wounded, bleeding, and gasping for breath, we have seen first-hand the destructive power of isolation. There is a basic reason for this: it is based on a lie. The falsehood that every lone ranger believes is that *no one else struggles like I do.*

Most men never realize that they are believing this lie, and yet almost every man does. This nasty lie eventually produces despair, and before long, the soul of another good man dies. The good news for all men today is the opposite of this lie. Although each man has a God-given uniqueness, our struggles with the flesh are typically the same. We are so similar because of the way God created us: just like Adam. We all struggle with the same monsters on a daily basis. Here are the big ones that connect us deeply as brothers:

- Fear
- Lust
- Insecurity
- Selfishness
- Sadness
- Anger
- Resentment
- Envy
- Critical attitudes

Sound familiar? Are you a male who is still breathing? If so, you will struggle with every one of these issues—and more. Every man that you know is also struggling with these forces. Your pastor, your next-door neighbor, and your co-workers are experiencing this universal pain. We are all in the same battle together. The truth of the matter is that each man's struggle is every man's struggle.

Mutual Support

When Jim showed up at our men's meeting one Tuesday night, you could sense he had a heavy heart by the sorrowful look on his face. When I opened the floor for anyone who wanted to share, Jim quickly spoke up. "Yesterday I was discouraged after a rough day at work," he said with a catch in his voice. "I went home and went straight to my shop and drank a twelve-pack of Bud Light. I stood out there and hid from my family the rest of the night. But all day long guilt has been tearing me up. I don't want to go back to being the old Jim."

There was a long silence as the other men soaked up Jim's confession. From the looks on their faces I could tell they admired his humility. Finally, after looking at Jim, Pete spoke up: "I screwed up three days ago myself. I got drunk on vodka and yelled at my wife. I confess my sin to you guys and ask for your help."

Looking back at Pete and nodding, Jim declared, "I will do whatever it takes to help you, brother. You are not alone. We will fight together, and we will win together."

The passion and spiritual atmosphere in the room went through the roof that night as the love and commitment expressed by Jim and Pete for each other made a powerful impact. I tear up just thinking about it. This is the brotherhood in action. There is always a divine appointment when men come together and get spiritually transparent. Your battle is my battle. My pain is your pain. Our temptations and strongholds become a strong glue that cannot divide God's army.

We like to tell newly initiated men how crucial it is to stay connected at all costs. We are not being overly dramatic when we declare: "Without the brotherhood we die!" This is the truth. The battle for our hearts is too intense. There is only one ending to a man's story if he chooses to fight alone. He will spiritually die-- alone. This truth must be lived out in the day-to-day through the camaraderie found among men who literally have each other's back. Men who don't care about how they "look" or who knows the truth and might wield it against them as a weapon. Authenticity only comes through personal relationships, not a special book, video series, or program.

Too many folks are looking for the latter, like the pastor from our area who had heard scuttlebutt that God was doing something significant among the men in our region. After several men shared powerful testimonies with him, his curiosity got the best of him, and he called me to get the scoop. One of the first questions he asked: "What curriculum is your ministry using?"

I had to be honest, so I told him these three things:

1. We are not a ministry.
2. We don't use a curriculum.
3. We are simply experimenting with the Great Commandment to love God and each other.

The phone call did not last long. This pastor was looking for a program that his men's ministry pastor could quickly implement, but there was nothing I could do for him. The revolution that Jesus started was not a ministry program. Jesus did not use the newest curriculum with the twelve disciples.

Sparring Partners

By now, you may be asking, "What exactly happens when you brothers come together?" I'm glad you asked. We call it SPARing. I will explain in depth the four main activities we practice when we come together, but first, I want you to get the big picture.

Imagine an old-time boxing ring and a champion middleweight boxer climbing into the ring. Alongside him is a buddy, who is in the same weight class. The two athletes begin to spar, holding nothing back. I'm talking 100 percent, with fierce grunting, sweating, and punches flying. These guys are serious! After an intense, hour-long sparring session, both men are spent. They have nothing left. In total exhaustion, they smile at each other, embrace, and head to the locker room.

Consider this scene before you answer the question: What was the goal of these two men in the ring? Although it may have appeared like a fight, they had no desire to harm each other. Each had the same basic purpose: to give all they had and leave the ring stronger. They wanted to empower each other, which is the essence of sparring. Our objective is to do whatever it takes to help each other be the best husbands, fathers, and leaders we can be. Like those middleweight boxers, we hold nothing back as we give 100 percent. We sweat and exert ourselves. Not physically, but spiritually.

Practically speaking, there are four unique relational activities we are committed to live out with one another. We spell them out using this acronym: S-P-A-R. In this chapter I will review the first letter, S, and the remaining three in the next two chapters.

Sharpening One Another

The S stands for SHARPENING, in the spirit of Proverbs 27:17: "As iron sharpens iron, so one man sharpens another" (BSB).

Often, when I speak to a group of men, I ask, "Who wants to be spiritually sharp? Raise your hand." Almost all hands go up. But when I ask the follow-up question, "Who wants to endure the pain of being spiritually sharpened?" only a few hands stay in the air. Why is iron sharpening iron such a rare activity? Because it hurts! I would much prefer watching a football game with my buddies or going bass fishing. Like most men, I don't like pain.

One of my best memories with my son involved spending an entire day with a blacksmith named James, who had more than thirty years of professional experience. We arrived at his house at 8:00 a.m., hoping to take a rusty old tire iron and transform it into a rugged, hunting-worthy buck knife. We planned to go at it the old-fashioned way, with a small rustic forge, an anvil, and a hammer.

That day, we spent close to eleven hours pounding on this piece of iron, throwing it into the fire, letting it cool, and beating it again.

While we were merciless, when we were done, we had the strongest knife around. I can't say it measured to the precision of the legendary Buck Knives that are known nationwide. And while it may not have been the most beautiful knife, I would put it up against the strongest production knife manufactured.

Give me your best knife and chances are that I can find a way to break it. I guarantee that you can't break the knife my son and I pounded out. We experienced genuine, sweaty, grueling iron-sharpening-iron reality that day. Like smashing a boxer silly, we hammered, beat, and pounded, knocking off every piece of iron that didn't belong until we were left with a razor-sharp buck knife. We did whatever it took to get the job done.

We desperately need this kind of relational intensity as men. We need men to love us enough to sharpen us—to pound on us with the love and truth of God. How do we do this? We ask probing questions and continue until a man gets to the root of his issues. Not too long ago a guy named Terry was experiencing considerable pain in his marriage. His brothers asked him these four questions:

1. What resentment do you have toward your wife?
2. What selfish expectations do you have toward her?
3. What is she needing from you right now?
4. What fears do you have as a husband?

It is miraculous what the Holy Spirit can do in a man with a few simple questions—the kind of probing questions that will crack open a man's heart. Terry knew in his head what it took to have a good marriage. He not only believed the Bible's teachings on marriage, but he also attended a marriage conference with his wife earlier in the year. He knew that God wanted him to love his wife as Christ loves the church.

But the reality of Terry's spiritual health as a husband resided in his heart, not with the correct information ratting around his brain. An intellectual grasp of the truth was not enough. Terry had to see the truth of what was going on in his heart. That day, Terry found his voice. The more he spoke, the more his heart was revealed. He was shocked at what he discovered: he was clinging to unforgiveness. His wife had spoken words of disrespect three weeks earlier, and Terry was still stewing over it. Yet he had no idea of how that resentment had been robbing him of marital peace. That day he recognized that his problem was not his marriage—it was him!

Risky Feedback

There is a second way that we brothers sharpen one another: by giving feedback. This meets the spiritual growth pattern spelled out in Ephesians 4:11–15, which says Christ himself gave us apostles, prophets, evangelists, pastors, and teachers to build up the body of Christ and help us mature. This passage includes a challenge in verse 15: to speak the truth in love. Sounds simple? Not necessarily. It's always risky to give a man feedback, never knowing if he will receive it graciously and with gratitude, or blow up in anger.

One time I had a rather intense telephone discussion with Tom, one of my spiritual mentors. Before we hung up, Tom said, "Can I give you some feedback?"

"Sure thing," I replied, trying to act nonchalant as my nerves jangled on the inside.

"At times you can be arrogant and talk too much," Tom said.

Although I thanked him for his words, when I hung up the phone, I felt furious. What an insult! A couple hours later, my emotions died down. As I headed down the road, a still small voice whispered, "Tom was right." Talk about pain. I immediately recognized the Holy Spirit's correction. While His rebuke stung, the next day I told a buddy named Todd about the painful truth that had hit me like a sledgehammer. I asked Todd to help me with my arrogance.

Why is feedback so crucial in the brotherhood? Because it helps us appreciate our blind spots. We all have them. Every day good men do stupid things, which prompts the question: what are the top three blind spots in your life? Think carefully. A seemingly stupid question, right? If they are blind spots, you have no idea what they are! Our blind spots, or areas of deception, are a part of our weakness. They can cause destruction in our lives if they don't come into the light.

This is where the brotherhood comes to the rescue. The powerful thing about the body of Christ is that we can see each other's blind spots and alert friends to them, even as we can't see our own. Yet to reach spiritual maturity, it is crucial that we reach out and remove each other's blinders. Even if it hurts. There is a powerful truth in Proverbs 27:6 that says: "Faithful are the wounds of a friend; but the kisses of an enemy are deceitful."

This is a perfect description of sharpening. Just like James, my blacksmith friend, there is a lot of fierce pounding that goes on in our brotherhood. Sometimes we get pretty beat up. Sometimes we totally miss the mark with our feedback. Sometimes we speak the truth, but love is in short supply. As you may imagine, when it comes to painful situations, tender emotions, and long-buried problems, things can get messy.

Still, at the end of the day, we know that we are deeply loved by brothers who are committed to our well-being over the long haul. Do you have any brothers in your life who love you enough to expose your blind spots?

Man of Courage

King David had a man in his life who was not afraid to speak the truth: the prophet Nathan. God sent Nathan to speak truth to David and convict his heart over his sin of adultery with Bathsheba and the resulting murder of her husband, Uriah, one of the king's closest military leaders. Think about that for a moment. King David, a man after God's own heart, was unaware that betrayal of a top aide, adultery with the man's wife, and murder were a big deal. Do you think he had a few blind spots?

Let's pause for a moment to consider Nathan's courage in this situation. In this era, kings were all-powerful and all-mighty. Tick the king off badly enough and you might lose your head in the process. Nathan had no idea how David would react to what he was about to say. He literally risked his life when he stepped forward to look David in the eyes and deliver the painful truth.

Nathan didn't mince words or try to be tactful either. He faithfully wounded David out of obedience to the Lord, telling him what God had said: "I anointed you king over Israel, and I delivered you from the hand of Saul. I gave your master's house to you, and your master's wives into your arms. I gave you all Israel and Judah. And if all this had been too little, I would have given you even more. Why did you despise the word of the LORD by doing what is evil in his eyes? You struck down Uriah the Hittite with the sword and took his wife to be your own. You killed him with the sword of the Ammonites. Now, therefore, the sword will never depart from your house, because you despised me and took the wife of Uriah the Hittite to be your own" (2 Samuel 12:7–10).

Re-read those words and see if you can feel the sting of Nathan's message from God. In this moment, David demonstrates why the Lord called David a man after His own heart: "Then David said to Nathan, 'I have sinned against the LORD'" (v. 13).

I love this passage because it portrays how ridiculously clueless men can be—thoroughly blind to obvious weaknesses and glaring sins in our own life. Such blind spots can derail us in life and in personal relationships if we don't have a Nathan willing to blow the trumpet of truth in our ear.

This is the essence of sharpening: asking probing questions and speaking the truth in love. I have seen both tools used by God to save a man's soul, his marriage, and his destiny. We all must be sharpened by godly men who care deeply for our hearts. We must also love our brothers enough to sharpen them in return. There will be pain involved. Guaranteed. Are you willing to endure the pain of brotherhood?

CHAPTER 7

Being Brothers: Praying and Affirming

Back in 2018, before world events, political fortunes, and the shifting tides of history affected their respective positions, *Forbes* magazine named Russian strongman Vladimir Putin and then-U.S. President Donald Trump as the two most powerful men in the world. By 2021, now-Citizen Trump had slipped to third place, with China dictator Xi Jinping rising to the top position.[1]

There is no doubt all three of these men have considerable influence around the world, but are they powerful in the purest sense of the word? If you could be any of these leaders in the blink of an eye, would you do so? Probably not.

If you are a believer in Christ, you have something in common with this trio. You are power-hungry. But don't worry, this is not a bad thing. It is simply how God created you. As men, we have a healthy hunger for power because we desperately need it. However, the power that our masculine hearts crave has nothing to do with wealth and self-promotion.

As men of God, we have much at stake—every day of our lives. We have a serious calling as husbands, fathers, leaders, and ministers of the gospel. There is darkness to be conquered and captives to be liberated. If we are going to succeed in the adventure of manhood, we need power, and a lot of it.

We need genuine power, not the fabricated, impotent kind that we see exhibited by Hollywood stars, media celebrities, and heads of states. The brotherhood needs the real thing, the power of almighty God. We cannot live without it. Without genuine power, we might as well replace our SPAR meetings with tea parties.

Power of Prayer

Where does this "God power" come from? Prayer—the P in the S-P-A-R acronym. This does not mean we turn every SPAR session into a prayer meeting. In fact, we don't host many prayer meetings. For us, PRAYER in the brotherhood simply means, as I like to say, "Allowing God to do and say whatever God wants to do and say in His men and through His men for His purposes and our freedom."

I can imagine some readers saying, "Sure. Another cliché." But it's not. We're so serious about this that some SPAR groups place an extra chair in the room. It's a tangible reminder to every man that God is alive, present, and ready to move mountains! Jesus put it this way: "For where two or three gather in my name, there am I with them" (Matthew 18:20).

We recognize how easy it can become for a men's group to fall into a rut of story-telling and forget that God is ever-present, ever-powerful, and ready to do miracles. This is what makes a SPAR meeting different from most men's small groups. God is the most important Man in the circle, and He remains top priority from the beginning to the end.

How does prayer show up in SPAR? We do prayer differently than many men have experienced in other small group meetings. Some say we do prayer backwards. The reason? When a man shares his situation or his spiritual need, we refuse to pray for him.

"What?" you might say. "What kind of friends withhold prayer when a man is in need?"

Well, we believe there is a better way. Instead of praying for him, we lead the man into an intimate God encounter by asking the man to voice his need honestly to God.

Take Steve, who was then struggling in his relationship with his rebellious sixteen-year-old daughter. We could have laid hands on him and prayed, asking that God help him be a strong dad or change his daughter's behavior. But we didn't. We asked him to find his voice and express his pain and struggle out loud. We also asked him to confess to God the specific fears he had in his relationship with her. Steve put a voice to both requests in prayer; the pain in his voice resounded throughout the room.

At this point, God was at work powerfully in Steve's heart. Sensing the power of the Holy Spirit doing His work, we asked Steve to confess the lies that he had been believing about his daughter's heart and God's faithfulness towards his daughter. He followed our lead.

The next part of this encounter was the most important. We asked Steve to be silent and simply listen. By now, genuine repentance (change of mind) had taken place. In the presence of the Lord, Steve began to see things the way God sees them. When he did, Steve's heart toward his daughter began to soften.

After a period of silence, we asked Steve what truths God wanted him to deeply know. He paused and finally said, "I have been believing the lie that says I am a terrible father. This lie came from past mistakes of neglecting my kids when I worked long hours. I realize today that I am a good dad because God says I am. Because of Christ, I love and lead my children well. I will not give into shame any longer. God is big enough to help me love my daughter during this difficult time!"

Transformed Men

During this session, three of us stood around Steve, amazed as we witnessed the transformation that took place in him within fifteen minutes. Although it was a simple conversation between a dad and Father God, it was evident that we had just witnessed real power in action. A power that changed Steve's heart! In fact, we were all changed when God's power showed up simply and quietly that day. His power usually does when you approach Him with honesty and true hunger.

Before ending our session, we asked Steve to say a prayer of thanksgiving for the beautiful daughter that God had given to him. As Steve gave thanks for all of the good attributes in his daughter's heart, tears streamed down his face. I shed a few tears as well while praying a prayer of gratitude for my own daughter.

Do you see the difference between "praying for a brother" and "leading him to encounter God?" The great thing about God is that I get to encounter Him directly, be gut-level honest about my pain and need, and then listen to Him speak the exact words that my heart needs to hear. This is true no matter what church, denomination, fellowship, or background you claim. It is good to have brothers who can help me have the "God conversation" that I desperately need.

Did you notice that in Steve's encounter, the most important part was listening? Conversation goes both ways, but the priority should always be on God's voice. John 8:32 says: "Then you will know the truth, and the truth will set you free." This isn't referring to a mere understanding of Scripture but a deep, intimate knowing of the Lord. And only the Spirit of God can move His truth from our heads into our hearts. In our brotherhood, we desperately need to hear God's voice of truth. Without it, we are sunk.

The one question that I ask more than any other when talking with one of the men is: "What is God saying to you?" It's my favorite question to ask any man, regardless of his circumstances or the condition of his heart. I know that God is always faithful to speak to His sons, and if we choose to listen to Him and receive from Him, transformation of the heart will follow.

In a SPAR meeting, we receive God's Word through the Bible, other brothers, and the Holy Spirit. Of course, all three sources must line up with biblical truth. If I had to choose my favorite mode of delivery, it would definitely be the Bible. There is no greater way to hear God's voice of truth clearly and accurately than to open the Scriptures. Paul told Timothy to be "a worker who does not need to be ashamed and who correctly handles the word of truth" (2 Timothy 2:15).

However, I must make an important distinction. SPARing is not a Bible study. Although we love studying God's Word in our personal quiet time, this is not our focus when brothers come together. When we open the Bible, we allow God's Word to do what God intends. We respect the words of Hebrews 4:12:

For the word of God is alive and active. Sharper than any double-edged sword, it penetrates even to divide soul and spirit, joints and marrow; it judges the thoughts and attitudes of the heart.

Knife-Like Precision

We let God's Word do its perfect work. We allow it to cut like a knife. We allow His words of truth to open our hearts and perform needed surgery. While it is painful, it is a good pain. Why do we need our "thoughts and attitudes of the heart judged" by God's truth? Because at times our thoughts and attitudes can be wrong, selfish, and even evil. We are often dead wrong in how we view our lives, God, others, or the world. Proverbs 14:12 reveals how easily we can be deceived when it says, "There is a way that appears to be right, but in the end it leads to death."

This means our only hope for righteous living is utilizing the sharp instrument of God's truth to correct our spiritual eyesight and restore us to peace and wholeness. This only happens when we humble ourselves and by faith receive His truth.

In practical terms, how does this happen in a SPAR meeting? It is a simple, two-step process. First, we read God's Word aloud. Second, we respond; the key is responding. Many men miss this all-important part while getting caught up in discussing, understanding, teaching, and listening to the Word. But let's be honest, the main thing is a childlike response, back to God Himself, from a humble heart.

Remember, prayer is simply a conversation with God. When God speaks (through His Word and His Spirit), it is our privilege to respond (through simple, honest prayer). This is the highlight for most men in a SPAR meeting. Don't get me wrong. I enjoy probing questions, giving feedback, and affirmation. But nothing compares to the transformation that happens when I speak out loud to God in response to His Word.

Recently, a brother named Ken was struggling financially because his sales commissions had been decreasing for several months. It grew so bad that he couldn't see much hope for anything different moving forward. God spoke His incredible truth in Philippians 4:19, "And my God will meet all your needs according to the riches of his glory in Christ Jesus."

Even after Ken read this verse aloud, he still felt stuck. But everything changed when he bowed his head and began to converse with loving Father God. Ken asked God to forgive him for the sin of doubt and unbelief. He confessed believing the lie that said, "Work harder, Ken! It's all up to you." He realized that God will always meet his financial needs, and there is no need to worry about his checkbook—ever. Ken raised his head, opened his eyes, and smiled with great relief. Once again, God met a man powerfully in the place of prayer

The Key

The P in SPAR is truly what makes or breaks a meeting. Sometimes brothers will spend too much time talking to one another and . . . time slips away. Before they realize it, ninety minutes have passed and it's time to go home to their wives and kids. The meeting was good, yet they didn't encounter Father God in the powerful place of prayer. SPAR is lacking unless we spend time hearing God's truth and responding to His voice.

Intimate prayer in the midst of caring brothers is where we experience the transformation that we need the most. Some men are reluctant to participate in the brotherhood's simple, vulnerable form of prayer; they realize that much of their public prayer has been guarded and somewhat mechanical, like someone offering a "thank you for the food" swipe at their obligation.

Our simple advice to these guys can be summarized: pray as if you are the weakest man in the room. This goes back to our greatest attribute as men—weakness. Even on our best day we are desperately needy. The greatest gift of our weakness as men is that we know the truth: we can do NOTHING without God.

Did you know that it is impossible to have a prayer life unless you are overwhelmed with your weakness? A man confessed to me one day that he was struggling being disciplined in his prayer life with his morning quiet times being nearly non-existent. He felt guilty that he could go all day long and not pray at all. Looking him in the eye, I replied, "Congratulations! You are self-sufficient, talented, and able to make life happen in your own strength. You have no need for God. You don't need a prayer life!"

He got the point. His problem was not a lack of talking to God, it was his lack of needing God. A self-sufficient man has no need for God. As legendary British pastor and author C. H. Spurgeon put it, "We pray best when we are fallen on our faces in painful helplessness."[2]

This is what I love about the brotherhood: the same weakness that propels us into intimate relationships with one another is the same weakness that propels us into prayer so we can encounter the power of God. Vulnerable, conversational prayer is the cornerstone of the brotherhood.

Value of Affirmation

After prayer comes the third letter of S-P-A-R: AFFIRMATION, which is another vital, relational activity. When was the last time someone looked you in the eye and forcefully declared who you are in Christ? Affirmation is essential to living free. Free from the burden of unconfessed sin, guilt, or nagging situations that can be resolved when expressed to another, caring brother. Unfortunately, few men receive this gift on a regular basis.

Affirmation is crucial for a basic reason: the Big Lie. Not only do many men wrestle with it, but the Big Lie has killed the hearts of many a good man. The enemy of our souls whispers it constantly, "You do NOT have what it takes to be a man!"

Heard that one lately? You may have without even realizing it. If you are discouraged, angry, or fearful today, it could be that you are believing one of the many forms of this dastardly falsehood. Do any of the following sound familiar?

- You don't have what it takes to love your wife!
- You are a failure as a father!
- You have made too many mistakes for God to use you!

The Big Lie comes in all kinds of flavors. And once we believe the lie, we are knocked out of the ballgame. We are rendered powerless, impotent, and frustrated, lingering on the sidelines, hoping for a superstar to save the game. This is where the brotherhood comes to the rescue. We become the mouthpiece of God as we forcefully declare to one another, "You have what it takes as a man. You are a good husband. You are a powerful father. You are a righteous man of God."

We don't offer these as empty words, but affirming ones. We aren't at a pep rally and trying to arouse team spirit; we aren't giving out meaningless pats on the back or compliments. Neither are we teaching, preaching, or counseling; we are delivering truth to a man's deep heart. Truth is vital to the health of his spiritual heart. To slightly paraphrase Psalm 42:7, it is deep calling unto deep. It is a God encounter.

Affirmation may be the most powerful activity of our brotherhood.

Just one example involves John, who struggled with considerable shame for months after his divorce was finalized. Although he fought and struggled for years to keep his marriage alive, he still ended up holding that dreaded decree in his hands as his heart shattered into smithereens. Every day, John believed the painful lie Satan whispered to him: "You are a terrible husband."

This lie-based shame tormented him day and night. One night John showed up at one of our men's training sessions. One of our leaders, Steve, brought the truth into the light. Setting the stage for a showdown, Steve opened up God's liberating truth to counter this deceptive, nasty lie.

After a frank discussion of the issue, Steve boldly stepped onto John's spiritual battlefield and passionately declared: "John, you were a good husband! And today, you are a good husband! You *do have* what it takes to love others. And God has a wife for you that will have the ability to receive your love."

Those who don't believe in the power of divine transformation should have seen John that day. As he chose to believe the truth about himself, it destroyed the cloud of shame in an instant. God used an ordinary man, Steve, to deliver earthshaking truth to John. Three weeks later, John met a special woman. Seven months after that, he married her. Today, John is being the powerful husband that God says that he is—all because he started believing the truth about his identity in Christ.

Strong Support

This is the power of affirmation. It is so vital because the battle for the mind is intense. The battle for *my mind* is intense. The enemy will never stop hurling lies in my direction. He will always have another creative way he hopes to dupe me into believing I am not who God declares that I am.

Thank God that I am not in this war by myself! I have a crew of men who know the real me, and they take great joy in reminding me of who I am. I can hear the voices of my fellow warriors right now as I type: "You are a powerful husband, a loving father, and a righteous man of God!"

I need to hear these liberating truths from my brothers. Every day of my life.

CHAPTER 8

Being Brothers: Repenting

I will never forget meeting Gary. He was in deep pain and a no-show in his marriage and parenting. Gary was stuck in a deep pit with no idea how to get out. While his buddy Jeff had been encouraging him for a long time, Jeff knew that Gary needed more and made it a personal goal to get him initiated into the brotherhood. Gary resisted for a long time, but out of respect for his friend, he finally relented.

That's how I met him. Before long—in fact, before I introduced myself—I knew what Gary needed: the gift of repentance. It's what we all need on an ongoing basis. It also constitutes the fourth relational activity of S-P-A-R. Repentance is the ultimate goal when brothers come together.

It's not what most men think it is; it's not simply a change of behavior. Repentance is much heavier than confessing a sin and receiving forgiveness. It's far more than an outward display because it goes to a man's very heart and soul. The Greek word for repentance is *metanoia*, which means a "change of mind." Whenever a man's mind is changed, then his behavior is guaranteed to change.

Trying to persuade a man his life will be transformed if he just goes to church every week, prays, and reads his Bible is an exercise in futility. A man's life will only change when his mind changes. Repentance is a sincere, heartfelt, earth-shattering change of mind. But it won't just be a surface "How are you? Good to see you" Sunday morning shake of the hands. This change will be lived out all week long, at work and at home, where a man's family can see and feel the newness and transformation.

The sad thing is many Christian men have become skeptical that true transformation can happen for them. Too many have sat through countless sermons and yet remain trapped in sin and bondage. When this happens, they can become hardened as they go through the motions of daily Scripture reading and weekly Bible studies. This is a tragedy; true repentance can take place easily for any man willing to step out of isolation.

How does repentance take place? The first step is obvious: get initiated into a brotherhood! Once a man lets go of his last fig leaf, it exposes the truth and brings his *real* heart issues into the light. It certainly did for Gary. He had no idea that he had so much pain and darkness inside his heart. With some help from his brothers, he ripped off his masks for the first time in his life and stepped into the light.

Identify Heart Issues

The second step of repentance is simple: identify the heart issues. In Gary's case, this didn't take long. He readily confessed to regularly coming home from work, going straight to his man cave, and drinking a six-pack. He knew he shouldn't be escaping behind a beer and the TV set. It meant he wasn't acting like the husband he should be, nor the father his two little girls desperately needed. Trapped in a mysterious depression that Gary couldn't seem to shake, he felt hopeless. Isolated. Unfulfilled. Desperate.

Men like Gary are why we are so committed to helping guys dig deep and discover the root of their sin. Root sin is what is hidden deep inside the heart. Remember, it's all about the heart! Many men mistakenly think that sin is:

- Disobedience
- Wrong choices
- Evil thoughts or actions

While these may be the bitter fruits of sin, they miss what every business owner likes to call "the bottom line." God gives us His clear-cut definition of sin in Romans 14:23: "Everything that does not come from faith is sin." In other words, sin is simply the refusal to not believe God and His powerful promises. It is a life lived without faith in God.

Hebrews 11:6 says: "Without faith it is impossible to please God, because anyone who comes to him must believe that he exists and that he rewards those who earnestly seek him."

Faith. God simply desires His children to trust him. The best way we can serve one another in the brotherhood is to help each other with our faith—or lack of faith. The easy way to do this is to empower one another to see the stupid lies we might be believing. The lies we believe are the real obstacles in our lives and set into motion all our unwanted behaviors.

As the group talked with Gary and he went deeper into his story, we learned of an incident that had happened three years earlier. He had been frequenting a bar for a while, and as so often happens in this kind of loose morals environment, developed a seemingly harmless, casual friendship with a cute female named Tammy.

One night, feeling frustrated and lonely, Gary accepted Tammy's invitation to go to her home, where they had sex. A moment of pleasure produced long-lasting guilt. The next day he felt terrible. He was shocked, angry, and confused by his behavior. He felt so horrible about it he finally confessed to his wife. Naturally, she was deeply wounded, but turned to God and found the strength to forgive him.

Overcoming Shame

However, long after this event, we were looking at a shell of a man. His primary heart issue: he was filled with shame. Before going any further, let's observe the definition of shame. It has nothing to do with past sins that you have committed, or grievous acts that were committed against you. Our past has no power in our lives now because the cross has conquered all sins. Instead, shame comes from the lies that we believe about ourselves today. Gary believed a huge lie about his identity, which created debilitating shame. Now, he had confessed the outward sin of adultery, but he hadn't been set free from the big one: shame.

Looking closely at Gary, I asked if he felt shame over his act of adultery. He nodded. I wasn't surprised; I could see it in his eyes. Then I explained that shame is nothing more than believing a lie about who we are as men. To help Gary escape this plot, we asked him to kneel before God and then asked him the big question: "What lie are you believing today about who you are?"

Head bowed, Gary knelt in silence. Finally, he confessed, "I have been believing the lie that I am worthless." For him, it was a shocking revelation; he had no idea the pain he had been feeling was connected to a lie that he had carried around like a monster on his back. This is the power of lie-based thinking. It destroys the life of Christ in us. Believing a lie is the essence of sin. Having no idea that he had embraced a dastardly falsehood, Gary was clueless that his pain was the fruit of a simple lie.

This realization set the stage for the third step, which is simply receiving God's truth. This is where the Holy Spirit "struts His stuff," and Father God cuts loose with a huge fireworks display in the heavens.

This is where a man is truly set free. It is important to know that we cannot help a man believe, which should set you free as a discipler. We can help a man break out of isolation and help him identify the issues of the heart, but we CANNOT help him receive and believe God's truth. Only God can do this. John 16:13 says that "when he, the Spirit of truth, comes, he will guide you into all the truth." The Holy Spirit is incredibly good at persuading us of the truth that we need in the moment that we need it.

While Gary was still kneeling at his make-shift altar, I asked him the last question: "Who does God say that you are?" Once again, he remained silent for a while. Suddenly, without warning, a flood of tears exploded from his eyes as he passionately declared: "I am valuable in the eyes of God, completely accepted by Him. I am totally forgiven and worthy of God's love. I am a good husband and a good father!"

Escaping the Trap

Gary was set free that day. No more shame. No more emotional pain. No more beer binges. No more neglect of his wife and daughters. Because he received the gift of repentance, he experienced a genuine change of mind, which led to a radical change of behavior. His sin was no different than my sin. At times, we all choose unbelief and embrace a lie, which always leads to destruction.

It took a group of men to help Gary find freedom. God has brought a lot of men like him our way. None of us can make this journey on our own, which is why Paul advised: "Be devoted to one another in love. Honor one another above yourselves" (Romans 12:10). I wonder how many more years Gary's wife would have persevered, if he hadn't altered the unloving behavior that flowed from his shame-hardened heart?

What happened with Gary isn't a solitary, unique event. There is nothing more thrilling to the brotherhood than when a man expresses genuine repentance. It is a gift that we will always need, and one that God always delights in giving us. Let's face it, we will always struggle with unbelief because it is built into our humanity—the fleshly weakness that comes with being born into a sin-scarred world. And yet, there is always another opportunity to experience a change of mind and to find faith once again.

A man who had witnessed profound transformation in several men in the brotherhood asked me recently if you needed a counseling degree to help men find freedom. Laughing, I replied, "No. It's really quite simple. Just help a man see the lies that he is believing, and then trust that God is big enough to overwhelm him with the truth." If you want to help a man experience repentance, just ask him these three questions:

1. What is your struggle right now?
2. What lie are you believing?
3. What truth does God want you to receive?

It is thrilling to watch God do the heavy lifting in helping a man experience a transformational change of mind, which can happen in an instant. You don't have to wait years for a man to "peel off the layers of the onion." But remember, spiritual growth requires the help of others. If you need help, are you willing to ask other brothers for it? Are you willing to be used by God to help that brother who needs to experience true freedom?

The Four Basics

S-P-A-R. Sharpening. Praying. Affirming. Repenting. These are the four basic activities that take place in a biblically-based men's movement. If they sound simple, it's because they are. The Kingdom of God was created for the simple man; no experts or theologians are needed.

The best part about SPAR are the two attributes that a man must possess to spar with other men. Paul outlines these qualifications in Galatians 5. You may recall that Paul was full of holy anger towards the believers in the church of Galatia because they had heaped a ton of non-essential doctrines on top of the wonderful gospel of grace. They were acting as badly as the Pharisees, who had taken Ten Commandments and multiplied them to more than six hundred laws and regulations. In seeking to follow a rules-keeping, legalistic form of faith, they had lost the essence of Christianity by taking on the burden of self-reliance and self-effort.

Paul was attempting to open their blind eyes, letting them know that whether they were passionate about their faith or not was totally irrelevant. He cuts through all of their Christian clutter with this declaration in verse 6: "The only thing that counts is faith expressing itself through love" (v. 6)

Five simple words. *Faith expressing itself through love.* This is the bare essence of SPAR. When brothers come together, they exercise radical faith on behalf of each other, and this always expresses itself in transformational love toward one another. FAITH. LOVE. These are the only two qualifications for SPAR because they are the only two New Testament attributes needed to live the Christian life.

As I said earlier, I love the church, which is God's creation and instrument to reach the world. But the modern church has complicated discipleship with its numerous curriculums and a non-relational approach. The Bible has made it simple: we love others as Christ loves us. This is the essence of disciplining men.

We keep our approach to leadership simple, too. The most powerful leaders within the movement in East Texas are not talented preachers or licensed ministers. They are normal guys. What's not normal is their crazy faith that God still does miracles, which leads to a radical whatever-it-takes love for other men.

When I think of powerhouse leaders in our movement, I think of Greg, Jonathan, Marshall, Mark, and Jeff. Here's what they do for a living: garbage collector, door salesman, auto repairman, lawn maintenance worker, and asphalt layer. They remind me of the twelve ordinary guys that changed the world with Jesus Christ.

Congratulations! You have been officially equipped with enough knowledge to start sparring with the Christian men in your world. The real training begins when you meet up with your brothers this week. Please don't delay. What two men can you meet with for ninety minutes for your first SPAR session?

I challenge you to have the time, place, and the names of these two men nailed down during the next twenty-four hours. The men's movement needs to begin in your church if it hasn't already. Why not today? Why not with you and two of your friends?

There is one more thing that you need to know about partnering with a men's movement in your church, and it's pretty important. In fact, the whole movement hinges on this one thing: the brotherhood does NOT exist for you or your brothers. What does that mean? It's not about you! It is about . . . one more man.

CHAPTER 9

One More Man

With six Academy Awards, four Golden Globes, and a string of other honors to its credit, *Hacksaw Ridge* ranks in the top twenty highest box office attractions for World War II-related movies, pulling in more than $180 million worldwide.

This moving story portrays the ultimate purpose of our masculine army. It relates the inspiring account of Private Desmond Doss, who walked into the bloodiest battle of World War II without a weapon—only his faith in God. Desmond was a devout Seventh Day Adventist and conscientious objector, whose convictions prompted considerable ridicule and doubts about his supposedly cowardly reasons for not wanting to fight. Finally, Uncle Sam allowed him to serve as a medic, although he maintained his insistence on not carrying a weapon.

Desmond made history in April of 1945 on the Maeda Escarpment, a battlefield perched atop a sheer, four-hundred-foot-high cliff and fortified by hundreds of Japanese machine gunners and booby traps. The US Army's mission seemed impossible; when the pressure was too much for Doss and his fellow soldiers, commanders gave the order to retreat. But this brave medic refused to leave his fallen comrades behind. He ran alone into the kill zone repeatedly, single-handedly carrying wounded soldiers and lowering them down the cliff to safety.

His faith and bravery were insanely heroic, but what makes Desmond special to the brotherhood is a simple seven-word prayer that he prayed each time he saved another man's life. I have never forgotten his heart cry in the midst of a hellish battle. The words reverberate through my mind and those of so many in our brotherhood: "Lord, please help me get one more."

God answered this prayer over and over. By nightfall, Desmond had rescued seventy-five men. His fellow soldiers no longer ridiculed him for refusing to carry a gun. That day, he became a legendary hero. The East Texas brotherhood has adopted his prayer as our official creed. Every day we wake up and say, "Lord, please give us one more man. Just one more, Lord. One more."

This prayer request is not merely a slogan. It is a deep yearning, a passionate war cry to go after the next man who is trapped in pornography, selfishness, addiction, dead religion, or just plain boredom. Why? Because each one of us was once that man. We all have the same story. The gory details vary, but it's the same pain, sin, and misery of isolation. We will never forget that pain. And because an ordinary man chose to reach out to each of us and pull us out of our dungeon of isolation, we want to do this for another man.

We cannot keep the brotherhood to ourselves. We cannot hide the transformational power of SPAR. We MUST give it away. We must go after one more man.

Exciting Fulfillment

There is another reason we are passionate about finding the next man. Helping him find freedom in Jesus Christ is absolutely the most exciting, fulfilling, adrenaline-filled rush known to mankind. Next to loving our families, nothing else compares to laying our lives down for another man. Nothing. It is pure joy. Exciting. Fun. Just ask any man whom God has used to complete a rescue mission for one isolated man. You can get addicted easily.

One time I was helping at a Men's Bootcamp when I saw a new friend named Wayne. The first words out of my mouth were, "How is it going, loving your awesome wife?" His face lit up like a Christmas tree as he told me how his marriage had been totally transformed. I gave him a big bear hug as I recalled the pain and tears that had flooded from Wayne just eight weeks earlier.

Before we helped him escape from his traps, Wayne had been stuck in a pit of resentment and selfish expectations toward his wife. As you can well imagine, this dark cloud had sucked the life out of their relationship. The night the brotherhood helped him see the truth, Wayne repented of his sins, fell into the embrace of his Father God, and found freedom. Needless to say, his wife is thankful for getting a new husband and Wayne is ever-thankful for a few loving brothers who helped him see his sin. I'm thankful that God chose me to play a small part in it all.

I've encountered many similar scenarios. I particularly remember when Tom recently walked up to me during one of our camps with a somewhat dazed look on his face. It was the good kind, rooted in an explosion of joy in his heart. Choking back tears, Tom said, "I just helped a man get set free from the torment of unforgiveness!" I looked into his eyes and realized that Tom will never be the same again. When God uses you to change the trajectory of another man's life, you are hooked.

That day it was as if a switch had been flipped in Tom's heart, meaning he can never go back to life as he once knew it. Because of what happened, he will never be able to go back to what we like to call being a BCG: Bored Christian Guy. What exactly is a BCG? A committed, church-going man whose life consists of working hard and serving his family. He is a man of integrity, moral values, and rock-solid theology. He volunteers a few hours each week to church ministries or other activities. But sadly, the remainder of his time goes into his Big Pursuit.

The Big Three

For most men, the Big Pursuit comes from one of three different activities.

The first is CAREER. My friend, Joe Robinson—trainer, speaker, and founder of the Live to Work campaign—once wrote a brilliant book titled *Work to Live*. In it, he exposes the modern man whose primary passion is his job. This career-driven man derives most of his significance through his career; he thinks about work even when he isn't at work. His identity is closely connected to his chosen career. This is NOT normal. It is an American phenomenon, rooted in our addiction to achievement. We pride ourselves in production, promotion, and money. In essence, the crack cocaine of the average American man is success.

This is what makes America such a challenging place to live if you are a Christian man. Our culture is quite different from that of most other countries. In many European nations, a man has a balanced life. Never tempted to work more than thirty-five hours a week, he will joyfully use every day of his six weeks of annual vacation. The working man on the other side of the Atlantic has a much healthier relationship with his career.

What about you? Have you embraced the American idol of achievement? Does your life revolve around those forty-plus hours of work? Do you think about work when you are playing with the kids at night? Or do you work diligently at your job so that you may fulfill your God-given purpose on planet earth during the remaining seventy hours that you aren't asleep?

I've talked to countless older men who have poured their lives into their careers and achieved the cultural carrot of success and money available to everyone willing to work hard. All of these men wish they could have those thirty years back. Why? More than one has told me: "It was a waste. I chased a goal that wasn't worth chasing." While they don't regret the hard work, they are sad that they allowed themselves to be duped into making a job their Big Pursuit.

So why do so many men expend their primary energy in their jobs? Simple. We all want to have a sense of accomplishment. This isn't automatically bad; God has wired us this way. A godly man longs to accomplish something, but there is a far greater accomplishment for a man than workplace success.

Hobbies Galore

The second Big Pursuit is our HOBBIES. Every man has a hobby. Mine is the pursuit and cultivation of big largemouth bass. I have the privilege of managing a family-owned, fourteen-acre bass lake. I fertilize the lake all summer long, which ensures that all my bass grow as fast as possible.

I'm pretty avid about this. We try our best to harvest 600 bass per year, just to keep the lake healthy. Then there was the ten-pound lunker I had pursued since my youth. She had successfully avoided my lures for 31 years. That is, until the beautiful spring evening when a ten-pound, five-ounce bass hit my copper-bladed spinner bait with great force. What a thrill of a catch! The best part was that my good friend Paul was in the boat to watch it happen.

Not only are hobbies a great escape from the daily grind, they are the basis of father-son (or daughter) pursuits, a great way to enjoy time with friends, and emotionally replenishing activities, which are necessary for the care of the masculine soul. Maybe you enjoy working on your '57 Chevy, playing golf, deer hunting, tending your garden, playing video games, tinkering with electronics, or tying flies. Maybe your oasis is a woodworking shop, your Harley Davidson, or working out at the weight-lifting gym. Every guy can identify. But if any of these becomes the Big Pursuit, they can also be a total waste of a man's life. Which begs the question: Is your hobby your Big Pursuit?

Why do men go overboard with our hobbies? Simply because we find great joy in our personal passions; that's how God created us. A godly man will always look for an outlet that will allow him to express his unique passions. However, there is a passion planted deep within the heart of a man that is much more explosive than cars, guns, or physical fitness.

The Thrill of Victory

The third and final Big Pursuit is a weird cultural phenomenon: SPORTS TEAMS. And I don't mean getting exercise by playing in your city rec league or on your church's basketball team! I'm talking about the American pastime of eating potato chips while staring at a sixty-inch, high definition, surround sound, real-as-being-there TV set while screaming at a team of twenty-somethings with a ball in their hands.

Since I live about two hours east of the Dallas-Fort Worth Metroplex, I will give you one guess as to who we cheer for each Sunday afternoon. Right. America's team: the Dallas Cowboys! Whether you like the Cowboys, the Browns, the Eagles, the Giants, following professional (and college) sports has become one of the most passionate pursuits in the daily lives of Christian men.

It has also become one of the biggest money makers in the business world. Before the pandemic whacked the NFL's revenue down by 25 percent during 2020, the league was raking in $16 billion a year. Its latest TV contract, which runs through 2033, is worth $113 million. Starting in 2023, Thursday night games will air exclusively on Amazon (and over-the-air in the respective teams' markets), which paid a cool billion for the privilege.[1] Starting NFL quarterbacks are now multi-millionaires, as are many other players and the league's commissioner. Millions gather every week to watch the action.

Why do guys go crazy over eleven men trying to get a leather ball into the far end of a perfectly mowed pasture? Because we are wired for triumph. God has written onto our hearts a yearning to win and to experience the thrill of victory. There is nothing wrong with yelling at your TV on Sunday afternoons, but there is a thrill of victory that is much more satisfying than your team winning a Super Bowl.

Don't get me wrong. Neither career, hobbies, or following sports are wrong or ungodly. Lately, I have been in pursuit of a thirteen-pound bass to add to the state of Texas largemouth bass breeding program. I enjoy growing kale and peppers in my organic vegetable garden. I try to watch as many Texas Aggie football games with my dad as I possibly can.

Once again, none of these pastimes are bad. Not at all. The focus is these two words: Big Pursuit. What is your Big Pursuit next to loving your family? It's an important question to ask yourself. Be gut-level honest when you answer. You may be surprised, angered, or saddened to realize just how much of your life and passion is given over to meaningless, non-eternal activities.

Power of Brotherhood

The church is full of men who are literally wasting their lives, spending hours each week doing good things that have no eternal value, and bring no deep, lasting joy. Yet these guys are godly men, every one of them. They love Jesus and want their lives to glorify Him. So, what is the disconnect? Why are they throwing away their most valuable commodity: their time? Why are they not investing the remainder of their lives to build His kingdom?

The answer is simple. Good-hearted, church-going men are not experiencing the thrill of changing the world one man at a time like Jesus did because they simply don't know they can. Men are wasting their lives with stuff that will burn because they don't know any better. Nobody has helped them realize that they have what it takes to change someone's life and to deliver a miracle to the next man.

Sure, they have heard a ton of sermons on making a difference in the world, but it takes more than an inspiring sermon. They must have a band of brothers who will look them in the eyes and say, "You have what it takes to change another man's life." Each man must be convinced that the "Christ inside him" can change the history of heaven forever. This is the power of brotherhood. When a man becomes a vital part of a band of brothers, he joins an army that takes great joy in storming the gates of hell. This unique spiritual army is always moving forward, always setting another man free from boredom, bitterness, shame, and fear.

Oftentimes the men's movement that Jesus started doesn't get a lot of recognition because it's not an official "ministry," doesn't always meet in a church building, and happens too slowly, one man at a time. This revolution doesn't advertise, doesn't have a marketing budget, isn't looking for people's applause, and doesn't care about titles. Remember, the only thing that matters to this army of aggressive, yet humble, men is: *One more man.*

Desmond Doss, a simple army medic, made a huge difference. However, the truth is you and I get to accomplish something much more significant than this heroic soldier. While Doss physically rescued men from death at the hands of the Japanese, the brotherhood of Jesus Christ has the privilege of spiritually rescuing men from a destiny of apathy, destruction, and hell.

This is mind-boggling. We get to save marriages and children, revive passionless churches, and build vibrant communities. One man at a time. For the first twenty years of doing ministry, I did not aggressively pursue "one more man." The reason I didn't is that deep down inside, I didn't believe I had what it took. So, I played it safe and poured my heart into ministry activity. I preached about the revolution that Jesus began, but was too much of a wimp to play my part. I loved the thought of experiencing the zeal found in the Book of Acts, but I didn't have the faith to jump in. I was more passionate about speaking into a church microphone than loving a needy man.

To be honest, I was just another Bored Christian Guy, blinded to the earth-shaking power within me. But not anymore. After seeing more than a thousand men in East Texas transformed simply by destroying their isolation, I am convinced that a small, rag-tag band of brothers can change the world. And I deeply believe that, with all my weaknesses, I can be a vital part of this army.

World Changers

It doesn't matter if you are Baptist, Methodist, Church of Christ, Nazarene, Church of God, Lutheran, Episcopalian, or a passionate Pentecostal. We are seeing men of all denominations go from being pew-sitters to world-changers in one to three years. Once a man gets a taste of being a miracle-delivery man, his primary pursuits change in an instant. His business endeavors, hobbies, and favorite sports teams get demoted.

He no longer gets the same dopamine surge out of money, success, or a Super Bowl victory. Suddenly, the world doesn't look quite the same. His Google calendar begins to look different. He begins to use the valuable minutes of his day in new ways. Every day becomes an opportunity to multiply disciples, one man at a time.

I think of my good buddy, Mark. This guy has raised up more rock-solid, masculine disciples in East Texas than anybody else I know. He has spent thousands of hours, face to face with hungry men, and watched God do some really cool things in their lives and marriages.

But there is a crucial reason that his crown in heaven is going to be unbelievably huge. A number of years ago, Mark made a crucial decision in his life. He had just won the Texas state archery championship—a huge accomplishment—and saw the fruit of hundreds of hours of focused practice after shooting a bow for forty-two years. Although he enjoyed archery immensely and had a bright future in the sport, God spoke to him about his role in the men's movement, prompting Mark to take a long, hard look at his life. At fifty-four, what would be the best way to spend the rest of his years on this earth?

He made the painful decision to lay the bow down and use those hours each week to set men free. Today, Mark has no regrets about that decision. Instead, he has a great amount of joy about the hundreds of men he has helped find freedom in Christ.

I also think of my friend, Don. He had toiled for fifteen years in the family business and was set to inherit the company and millions in profits in coming years. But he gave it all up to become a full-time missionary to the local church and do just one thing: disciple the hearts of men. Don has zero regrets today, despite being totally dependent on God to pay his bills.

My sidekick, Paul, owned a successful company for thirty-seven years before selling it several years ago. One might think that he would have retired to enjoy his cattle farm in the country, but he is too busy relationally discipling marriages and men, one man at a time.

Not too long ago, I spent two hours with another true hero. He had just resigned from his job after eleven successful years, just so he could spend more hours each week discipling the hearts of men. When he took this step, he wasn't exactly sure how God would meet his financial needs. Although he has a wife and three young daughters, he has no fear. He knows God has called him to expand this men's revival into more churches in his denomination.

Greater Joy

Going after "one more man" is the greater joy. Yes, it is time-consuming, emotionally intense, and takes a lot of faith. It is messy and chaotic and always will be. But is there anything better to do with the few years that we have left on planet earth? Definitely not.

Take a look at your heart right now. If you are honest, you also have a yearning to be a part of a winning team, to accomplish something big, and find fulfillment in life. This is built into the soul of every man.

You don't necessarily have to quit your job, stop enjoying your hobby, or quit following your fantasy football team. Simply take a leap of faith and join the true world championship team called The Brotherhood. Look around your church, your neighborhood, and your workplace and find a man. Ask him to go fishing or just go have coffee with you, and then fiercely love him with the earth-shaking love of Jesus Christ. Enroll him into the greatest revolution ever. Then stand back and watch him change the world.

CHAPTER 10

How to Change the World

Charles was a man wracked by pain. On the outside, everything looked great: he had a wonderful wife, a young daughter, and a decent home, but his life was far from perfect. Primarily because alcohol was slowly destroying his marriage and his soul and contributing to an inability to keep a steady job. This all created monumental instability in his life. While mired in despair, Charles didn't have the guts to humble himself and cry out for help. So, his wife Rhonda did it for him.

It was the summer of 1995, during the peak of my full-time pastoral journey. I was passionate about being the best pastor the world had ever seen. After listening to Rhonda's story over the phone, I agreed to meet with Charles one sunny Monday afternoon. He held nothing back as he shared his pain, his fear of losing everything, and his guilt over being a poor husband and father. My heart broke for this man as he poured out his tale of woe.

After spending two hours together that day, we continued meeting weekly for the next several months. I counseled him with sound theology, listened with sincere interest, and felt true compassion for him. As I think back to that time and place, my heart was pure and my efforts sincere. But did I help this needy man? Not at all. I tried, but I didn't know the secret to powerhouse ministry.

My formal ministry training taught me to do one thing very well: verbally communicate the principles of God's Word, whether teaching, preaching, or counseling. I tried hard to be good at all three. But helping a man become Christ-like requires something different—the secret sauce to effective ministry: BROKENNESS. In those days, I was a prideful, unbroken man. A sincere man, yes. Saved, with Christ living in me. But I was unbroken.

There is nothing more powerful than ministry that flows out of a man's brokenness.

Until you allow your sin, past wounds, pain, and all of life's trials to crush you, then you will be of little value to the kingdom of God. Sure, you may be a brilliant Bible study leader, or the pastor of a vibrant, growing church, but the DNA of a fruitful minister will always be brokenness.

Ministering in Humility

Brokenness is so vital in reaching the world one man at a time because it produces a powerful attribute in a man. It's called HUMILITY. Nothing is more attractive than genuine humility. The absence of pride in a man makes him a magnet for others. I love to be around humble people because I always feel the freedom to be myself in the presence of a humble man. I open up and share things that need to come into the light. Humility cracks people open in amazing ways. In the brotherhood, we call humility the grand prize of all. It is our favorite attribute, and one we seek daily.

True humility is a powerful force because it causes us to CONNECT deeply with others. Without an intimate connection with another person, it is impossible to minister to him. I failed to help Charles in any meaningful way because I failed to connect with him. I showed up in the relationship as Mr. Capable Pastor while viewing him as the Needy Sheep. I was the teacher, and he was the student. Since I placed myself above him, we lacked any deep connection.

Today when I meet with a man, my perspective and approach is much different. My brokenness connects with his as his pain reaches deep into my own pain. My past mistakes shed light on his past mistakes. His struggles are merely a reflection of my struggles. In essence, we deeply connect because we are the same man.

That's right. Every man that I meet, regardless of how horrific their sin, or how messed up their life may seem, is absolutely no different than me. In the brotherhood, we like to say, "I am him, and he is me."

Regardless of who is standing in front of me, I am that man. We are one and the same. We are both in need of the grace and power of Father God. In my early days of ministry, I was blind to this wonderful truth. I hid my humanity, perverse thoughts, temptations, and sins from those whom I sought to disciple. I thought a good minister should focus on the needs of others, not his own. Well, I was wrong.

Do you see the progression I just spelled out? BROKENNESS gives way to HUMILITY, and humility creates CONNECTION. This process is the blueprint for genuine ministry. All of us must stumble down this bumpy path if we want to be used in God's kingdom.

"But," you may ask, "is this the essence of powerhouse ministry? Is this how the world is truly changed?"

Not exactly. These three steps are simply the precursors for the atomic bomb that does the real work of ministry. There is a Jesus force that flows freely from the fountain of brokenness, and it only happens when we deeply connect with other men in true humility. The atomic bomb that I'm referring to is agape LOVE.

Loving the Brothers

Believe it or not, the most important thing that we do here in the East Texas men's revival is deeply love the hearts of men. We have slowly and painfully learned to love others well. That's all. This may sound corny and shallow if you are a seminary-trained minister, and yet it is true. We have discovered that loving men like Christ loves us is miracle-producing and all-powerful. A man is discipled by the degree to which he is loved.

First Corinthians 13:1-3 says that there is something more powerful than having all knowledge, a faith that can move mountains, and a willingness to give everything to the poor. Essentially, it is the ability to love another person. I learned this the hard way as a full-time pastor. I loved "doing ministry" more than loving people. It still hurts to admit the truth. I thought I *was* loving people. I spent a ton of time with my church members, listening with compassion and serving with diligence. But I rarely unleashed the atomic bomb of love on anyone. I was a nice guy with solid theology, but there was little transformation in others' lives because of my connection with them.

I'm thankful God gave me another chance. My daily prayer today is, "God, teach me how to love others." It is the only thing that matters. It is also the most powerful force God has given the church to make disciples.

Some of you may still be doubting that love is the primary weapon that God's masculine army wields to transform the planet. Well, Scripture makes it plain to see. Let's look at two powerful biblical truths that explain how a man's heart is changed when he is supernaturally loved.

The first appears in 1 John 4:18, which tells us: "There is no fear in love. But perfect love drives out fear, because fear has to do with punishment."

Loving men with God's unconditional love destroys their fears. One of our greatest battles as men is fear. We can easily become fearful as husbands, fathers, workers, and leaders. In fact, most anger problems in the lives of men are simply expressions of fear, which shuts us down, immobilizes us, and causes us to love and lead poorly. What destroys fear 100 percent of the time? Love.

There's a second way that love transforms the masculine heart. First Peter 4:8 declares: "Above all, love each other deeply, because love covers over a multitude of sins."

Love covers all sins. This is huge. Next to fear, our greatest battle as men is condemnation. While it does come from the enemy, much of it originates within ourselves. We condemn ourselves for past sexual sins, loving our wives poorly, disciplining our kids in anger, financial failures, and more. I talk to men every day whose joy has been robbed by the shame of past failures. I believe that most of the depression men grapple with stems from self-condemnation. As with fear, it causes us to love and lead poorly. Love destroys this nasty foe.

This is the dynamic duo of agape love: freedom from both fear *and* condemnation. This changes everything. When a man is free from fear and condemnation, he can effortlessly be the husband, father, and leader that he desires.

Empowering Men

This is the essence of men's discipleship: empowering men by loving them deeply. This is the Jesus model of discipleship, which worked two thousand years ago and still does. Some churches struggle with this simplistic view of ministry, demanding the use of an expansive, robust curriculum to fully disciple their men. We disagree. While good theology is needed, the greater need is to empower men to radically obey God's Word alongside other men. Let's help men to experience the joy, as James 1:22–25 teaches, of being doers of the Word and not hearers only.

I know dozens of men who are changing the world using the relationship-based Jesus model of discipleship. These men have been broken because of past sins and hurts, but their brokenness is the best thing that they have to give another man. Men, marriages, and churches are slowly transforming because of these men.

One of these men has changed my life. His name is Greg. I will never forget my first encounter with him. Greg was one of the most obnoxious and rude men whom I had ever met. Today, he is radically different and one of the most powerful disciple-makers I know.

Greg's Story

Here is Greg's story, in his words:

"I grew up in an abusive home. My mom and dad were both alcoholics and drug addicts. Sometimes I was at home for weeks all by myself. My mom was constantly in and out of relationships with other men. One day she met a man named Tom. He was out of town most of the time, working in the oil fields. During these times, my mom would get lonely, drink heavily, and sexually abuse me.

"My life was hell. I felt trapped and had no way out. One day, at the age of eleven, I wanted to end my life. I was writing a suicide letter while in school, and my teacher found it. Unfortunately, the school called my parents and told them about the letter. That day, my mom choked me until I passed out. When I woke up, she did it again. She tried to force me to take a large amount of pills so I could go ahead and end my life.

"This led to the state of Texas removing me from my home and putting me in a foster home. Because of my hyperactivity, I cycled through many foster homes. There didn't seem to be a family that could handle me. Eventually, I was assigned to Azleway Boys' Ranch in East Texas.

"I was there from the ages of thirteen to eighteen and soaked up all of the attention. I did whatever it took to please others. It felt good to not be abused or rejected. But in reality, I was hiding and self-protecting. I was deeply wounded and lonely, but afraid to let anyone see my pain. I was afraid that they wouldn't like the real me.

"I went through many broken romantic relationships as a young man. I was looking for real love. I thought it could be found in the embrace of a woman. I thought that true intimacy could be found in a sexual relationship. Just after high school I found out that my girlfriend Emily was pregnant. I drove her to the clinic so that she could get an abortion. I helped to murder my own child.

"I was unable to hold down a job for very long because of my pain and anger. Finally, I wound up broke and homeless, and ended up living out of a tent that I had bought at Goodwill. Eventually, a friend's family gave me a bed and I got a decent job.

"At age twenty, things were looking up for me. But I was still broken and in much emotional pain. Then I met Julie. I think I fell in love with her sports car before I fell in love with her. We started having sex soon, and before long she was pregnant. And furious! She kicked me out of her life, gave birth to our baby, and I was back in a place of loneliness and despair.

"Somehow, I climbed out of that mess, got some needed training and skills, and started working my way up in the world. Eventually, I got a good job, married a beautiful gal, and seemed to be living the good life, at least from the outside looking in. We moved to Houston and I got my dream job, as an oil and gas executive. I was making a ton of money—and I was miserable. The deep wounds of my childhood continued to haunt me.

"I turned to alcohol. Although I hated the taste of beer and liquor, I loved the pain-numbing effects. I would fill a tall glass with vodka, topped with a small amount of orange juice, and chug it down. If I didn't pass out quickly, I would down another one. It got so bad that I was on the verge of losing my job. I immediately checked into a residential rehab center in central Texas. I came out of it delivered from my alcohol addiction. But, I was still totally screwed up. Then I began attending a Christian recovery ministry, but got mad at one of the leaders. I left and never came back.

"And then something happened that forever changed my heart and life. I met a bunch of guys who were different. Radically different. They gave me something that I desperately needed: unconditional love. These weak men gave me a safe space to be myself. They listened to my story. This brotherhood accepted me in the midst of my anger, confusion, bad theology, shame, and horrific sins. They showed me the real Jesus.

"When they did, I began to transform. God opened my eyes to the truth of who I am as His son. The last several years of my life have been a genuine miracle. Today, I am a new man. But, I have to tell you the best thing about this journey. I am thankful for all of the hell and the abuse that I have gone through during my life. The reason is simple. Every time I sit down with another man in front of me, I look him in the eyes and say, 'I know exactly how you feel. I have been there.'

"Today, I no longer have a desire to pursue success. In fact, I drive a trash truck and have never had more joy. My life is about loving my family and discipling one more man!"

Powerhouse Ministers

This is the bottom line of the men's movement that Jesus started: turning every pew-sitting man into a powerhouse minister. And it all begins with a man's brokenness. I have watched my friend Greg minister to many men. His ability to impact others is inspiring. Not too long ago, Greg and I were at a café when he noticed a man eating by himself. Greg asked if we could go sit down with the man. In less than sixty seconds this stranger was pouring out his heart about his recent cancer diagnosis. I watched in amazement as Greg dropped the atomic bomb of love on this man and breathed new life into him.

I recently met a guy who is a graduate of one of the best seminaries in North America. Bill has a razor-sharp mind and a deep knowledge of God's Word. He is also a great husband and father. I have the highest respect for this man.

Bill told me he had been wanting to use his knowledge to make disciples and God finally sent him a man named Ted. Bill met with Ted each week and got to know him at a deep level. It didn't take long to find out that Ted had a powerful addiction to pornography. Bill tried everything that he could to help him and began to lose heart that his friend would ever be free. His best friend, who happened to be a licensed counselor, told Bill that Ted seriously needed professional help. Bill agreed and reluctantly gave up on the man.

As I heard this story, I was painfully struck by the irony of it. Here was Bill, a man who had invested thousands of hours and dollars into learning the sacred truths of the glorious gospel of Jesus Christ at a prestigious seminary. He can preach and teach the gospel effectively. Yet, he was impotent when it came to applying the gospel to a real life need.

I also heard another minister (the senior pastor of a large church) make an interesting comment recently. His words were refreshingly different. He looked out at a large group of men in his church and said, "I no longer have to send any of our church members to Christian counselors. I just send them to all of you. Thank you for helping our church members find freedom in Christ."

The men in this Baptist church had proved to their pastor that they are capable ministers. Their pastor has seen dozens of transformed lives and marriages as a result of the East Texas men's movement functioning powerfully in his congregation. These men had learned how to drop the atomic bomb on men. They were committed to discipling the hearts of men in their church by loving them with great power, which flowed out of their own brokenness.

It took me many years to realize that ministry flows out of my weakness, not my strength. I tried for a long time to wrap my brain around the truth of 2 Corinthians 12:10: "When I am weak, then I am strong." Finally, I quit trying to understand it and simply accepted this life-changing truth.

Broken Men

Not too long ago I received a text from a man named Jim. His social media feeds had portrayed the perfect life: exotic vacations, good money, a beautiful wife, and successful kids. But his life told a much different story. His message read, "Can we meet? My wife left me two days ago."

Why did he reach out to me? Brokenness. I am a broken man. Thank goodness I am! I am grateful for every ounce of sin and pain that God has redeemed in me. I am proud of all my scars. I have already experienced the pain that Jim was now facing. He didn't need answers, therapy, or a pastoral visit. He needed a brother that could connect deeply with him. He needs the atomic bomb dropped into his life. And I get to deliver it. I get to love this man deeply. This is a great honor.

About a decade ago, when I was in the fetal position, not knowing if I was going to survive a hellish divorce, I had no idea that I was actually in God's seminary. I was fully enrolled in His training program for ministry: the School of Brokenness. I was being prepared to change the world. Because of divorce, I learned how to deeply mourn loss and disappointment. Now I get to help other men do the same.

Because of divorce, I learned how to forgive from the heart, when those whom you love sin against you and wound you deeply. Now I know how to help other men do the same. Because of my divorce, shame that haunted me for years came into the light. Through the blood of Jesus Christ, I became free from this torment.

Now, I pursue men who live under this same cloud of shame, and I lead them into freedom and identity in Christ.

Through the collapse of my marriage, I learned how to surrender. I lost almost everything that was meaningful to me. The only way I could find peace was to enter into a place of total surrender. Now, I get to lead other men into that same place. I may be a broken man, but I am proud of my brokenness. I boast about Jesus and what He has done in my life. I get to watch men be changed by the powerful Christ that is in me. All because I have been broken. I have been stripped down. I have become a Naked Warrior.

What about you? You may think that you don't have a powerful story like my friend Greg, but you don't need one. All you need is *your* story. Truth be told, your story is Greg's story. Why? Because your story contains the greater story—the story that every man needs to hear. It is the timeless story of Jesus Christ. The only question is: are you willing to tell your story?

Find a man. Tell him your story. Listen to his story. Your brokenness will connect with his brokenness. Best of all, God will show up in your midst. And you both will be changed.

CHAPTER 11

A Simple Challenge

Have you ever wondered what took place in the heart of the men who stood before Jesus and heard that terrifying, yet life-giving challenge: "Follow me, and I will make you fishers of men" (Matthew 4:19)?

How would you have responded? I can picture Jesus giving each man sixty seconds to give an answer. I bet He got a charge from the look of bewilderment on each face. I wonder how many men Jesus had to wade through before he found a team of guys crazy enough to give Him a "thumbs up"? Dozens? Possibly hundreds? All we know is that eventually he assembled a motley crew of twelve ordinary men—guys just like you and me.

What caused the disciples to give their life away to such a high-risk endeavor with a man who had a poor reputation, and leave behind the comfort and security they enjoyed? This was more than a leap of faith. This seemed to be insanity. Why did they sacrifice all, join a band of brothers, and sign up to change the world? *Because they were born for the challenge.*

Jesus touched something deep within these men that had never been touched before. They had been created for something with eternal significance. They didn't know what it looked like until they heard the Master's voice. When Jesus gave the invitation, they knew this was their destiny. They knew, without a doubt, that they were born for this.

You were too. Brotherhood and freedom fighting is etched into the fabric of your soul. Saying "yes" to the ultimate challenge is built into the heart of all men. When a man finds Jesus, he is fully wired to be a world-changer. Look at our modern-day US military: a force of approximately 1.3 million soldiers, sailors, pilots, and others—every person a volunteer. What did they sign up for? A whole lot of sweat, boredom, and tedious work. Very few get to experience the kind of excitement we see in *Hacksaw Ridge*. The paycheck isn't too great either. Oh, and one more thing: close to 85 percent of these enlistees are men!

These fine soldiers have enrolled into a noble and courageous cause: our physical freedom. While I should know better (especially since my son served in the National Guard), I often take it for granted that I get to live in a safe neighborhood, go to church where I desire, and have basic rights as a US citizen. I praise God for the members of our military, who stand guard night and day to protect our freedom.

But there is a nobler cause that exists for men to give up their lives. There is something greater than being armed with a weapon to protect against a possible Islamic terrorist threat. I'm talking about being fully engaged in the war for spiritual freedom! There are too many men who live in a nation known for its freedom who are not free. They may be physically, but their souls are in bondage. While sleeping safely in their homes at night, by day they are shackled with guilt and fear.

Where do you find these men? In your neighborhood, at your workplace, at the gym, and among the friends and relatives around your dining room table at holiday meals. Most of all, they are the men you see every Sunday morning in worship services. Who are the men in your local church who are not enjoying a life of spiritual freedom?

Think about every man that you know in your congregation right now: Which men struggled with pornography this past week? Which men are suffering because of marital pain? What are the biggest fears and struggles in the heart of your pastor today?

I will end this book with the all-important question that I ask every man in our community. Jesus knew the answer to this question: "Who are your twelve?" Do you know who God has called you to disciple? Your twelve are not a literal twelve men; the exact number is insignificant. What matters is the excitement of obeying God and giving your life away to a small handful of men, just like Jesus did.

There may be only two men whom you are called to disciple right now. Maybe it's four. Or seven. Remember, the number doesn't matter, only the hearts of the men involved. So, who are your twelve? Most importantly, how will you invest your heart and life into these men this week?

Most Christian men don't have this mindset. Most men in churches focus on what they do, not on who they are discipling. Ask any man, "What do you do?" and he will answer the question with ease. Ask a man in most any church "Who are your twelve?" and he will most likely go silent and stare at you with a strange look on his face. A simple question, but one that poses a challenge for most church-going men.

I wrote the contents of this book over the course of several years in three different states, sustained by dozens of pots of coffee, and empowered by the Holy Spirit, for one simple reason—to persuade each man who reads these words to find and disciple your twelve.

If you are a Bible teacher in your church, don't stop teaching. If you are a deacon, keep up your acts of service. If you are a singer on the worship team, keep on singing. If you are a youth worker, keep loving those teenagers. But, regardless of your church duties, to every man who confesses Jesus Christ as Lord, I ask you to go and make disciples. Disciple your twelve!

Do it like Jesus did, one man at a time, relationally, loving them deeply as you share your life and brokenness with them. Then help your twelve find their twelve and do whatever it takes to teach them how to love those men deeply.

If you do this, something amazing will happen. I guarantee it. It is the same phenomenon that occurred as a result of Jesus discipling His twelve. It is called "miraculous multiplication." The men that you relationally disciple will eventually cause a ripple effect across the planet, in the same way that the original twelve disciples turned the world upside down. They still are, two thousand years later.

It will start small. It always does. You disciple a man and his life changes. You get a phone call from the man's wife, thanking you for saving their marriage. Then it may slowly cascade down to impacting this man's friends and coworkers. Your twelve will eventually find their twelve. Momentum will begin to pick up.

At some point you will have no way of knowing how many men, women, and children have been transformed by the Jesus in you and your little band of brothers. The total of transformed people may number in the thousands and circle the globe several times. But the numbers will never matter to you because the joy comes from loving men and obeying God.

And then, many years down the road, the best part of the whole adventure takes place. You die (trust me, this is the best part of the story). After the death of your physical body, you end up in a place that your soul has longed for since the day that you were born again—heaven. You have finally made it to paradise.

In paradise God gives you a gift. He turns on a light switch and you finally see what God has been joyfully watching for many years: the ripple effect of discipling a small handful of men. He allows you to see the faces of all the people that were saved, transformed, and discipled as a result of the weak, yet powerful, efforts of you and your brothers. He then tells you exactly how many addictions were broken, how many divorces never occurred, how many suicides were prevented, and how many abortions never took place. This was Kingdom fruit that you never were able to see. But it happened, and all because you were faithful to disciple your twelve.

Your mouth drops open as you stare in amazement. It is a scene that is indescribable. How could this many people have been impacted by you and your small army of men? The real question is: "How could they not?"

I ask you to close your eyes and picture this scene in your mind right now. This mind-boggling vision is God's will for every man who confesses Christ. This is the life that you long to live. You were born to relationally make disciples, one man at a time, just like Jesus. It starts with one simple step of leaving isolation behind. Will you take the step?

Acknowledgements

This book is a celebration of the godly men in my life. I pen these words with much joy because of my gratitude for my brothers in Christ. Although I have had the privilege of writing the account of the East Texas brotherhood in hopes of fanning grassroots flames of men's ministries across the nation, there are hundreds of weak, powerful men who have lived it.

How I wish I could thank the dozens of men who have impacted my life for more than two decades. Each brother, unique in his brokenness and Jesus attributes, has loved me well. All these men have contributed something profound to my journey.

I will name four of these men. They are dear comrades who have walked with me through the deep trenches of life, love, and leadership for many years. This book is their life, which they live out every hour of every day. I have been transformed by watching them pray, suffer much, sacrifice for their wives, love their children, disciple the men in their churches, and transform their world. These men know how much I love them. Now I want you to know.

Paul Roberts was the first man crazy enough to jump into this journey with me. We have been on this road for more than twenty years. If it weren't for Paul's encouragement and steady hand, I would have given up on discipling men a long time ago. Every time that shame tried to destroy my calling, Paul looked me in the eyes and affirmed the powerful Christ that is in me. He believed deeply in me and kept reminding me of God's call on my life. A true brother will never let you stray very far from your destiny. Paul Roberts has always been just that to me.

My sidekick, Mark Alderson, is a real man if there ever was one. He has tirelessly worked to help me see my identity in Christ, an awakening that has changed my life. He also knows God's Word better than anyone else I know. It's not mere head knowledge, either; he lives it! I am constantly learning how to follow Jesus by watching Mark live his life. In addition, he also loves me enough to deliver painful feedback when I need it, including exposing a bit of poor theology in the manuscript of this book. I treasure every minute that I get to spend with this man. He is a true spiritual father to me. Thank you, Mark!

I'm not sure where I would be today without Jonathan Troyer. This man has a huge pastor's heart. Whenever I need a safe place to unload the sin and pain of my life, I run to Jonathan. God used this man to restore my soul when I was enduring the agony of divorce, when I told him things that nobody else will ever know. Every Wednesday at noon I have the privilege of sparring with Jonathan. His honesty about his pride, fear, and struggle to love his family gives me great courage. He always asks me the perfect question that exposes my heart, which creates a fresh hunger for Jesus. I am transformed by my Father God every time I meet with Jonathan.

Then there is my powerful brother, Paul Bolding. We met when Paul was a frustrated, full-time pastor. His transformation over the years has been mind-boggling; his fire to disciple the next man is unlike any other. He has taken the East Texas men's movement to the next level. I get to watch the world change because of Paul's faithfulness to God's Kingdom. But the best thing about Paul is his commitment to me. He loves me deeply and will do whatever it takes to help me be the best husband, father, and leader that I can be. He pursues me relentlessly, refusing to let me retreat to my cave. He has a passion for Jesus that is contagious. I love to be in the presence of Paul Bolding.

I also want to say a huge thank you to Ken Walker, my editor. Ken affirmed me every step of the way and helped me to see that I have what it takes to spread this message to the rest of the world. Many thanks for believing in me brother Ken!

Finally, thank you to every one of my SPAR brothers in Texas, Utah, Colorado, Florida, Oklahoma, and Arizona. Let's go get the next man!

About the S.P.A.R. Men's Movement

If you need assistance in launching a men's discipleship movement in your city or your church, just let us know. We love working with men and churches of all denominations. One of the best ways to get a taste of the Jesus Model of Discipleship is to participate in one of our weekend bootcamps. You can register at freedomtrainings. org. If you bring another man from your church, ask about our brotherhood discount. We have had almost 2,000 men go through our weekend training. It is a journey like no other!

We also have a large group of seasoned leaders that are more than willing to come to your church. Our team is ready to hop on a plane and head your way! Let us know how we can serve you and your church.

Thanks for taking the time to read our story. We are convinced that our entire nation can be turned upside down for Christ. One man at a time.

Brian Childres

Help us get the message out by purchasing books to give away!
Purchase through Amazon.com for $9.95 plus tax.
Bulk purchases can be made at wetrainmen.com.
3 or more books: $8.00 each
By the case (20 books): $135.00
THANKS FOR YOUR SUPPORT!

Endnotes

Chapter 4: Rites of Initiation

1. John Lynch, Bruce McNichol, and Bill Thrall, *The Cure: What If God Isn't Who You Think He Is and Neither Are You?* (Dawsonville, GA: Trueface, 2016), 23.

Chapter 5: Priority of the Heart

1. John Eldredge, *Wild at Heart* (Nashville, TN: Thomas Nelson Publishers, 2001), 64.

Chapter 7: Being Brothers: Praying and Affirming

1. *Forbes*, "The World's Most Powerful People: 2021," https://www.forbes.com/powerful-people/list/, accessed March 22, 2021.

2. C. H. Spurgeon, *C. H. Spurgeon Prayers* (London: Forgotten Books, 2016), 146.

Chapter 9: One More Man

1. John Breech, "NFL's new TV deal will bring some major changes," CBS Sports, March 19, 2021, https://www.cbssports.com/nfl/news/nfls-new-tv-deal-will-bring-some-major-changes-here-are-10-things-to-know-including-flex-games-on-monday/#:~:text=If%20you%20missed%20it%2C%20the,runs%20through%20the%202033%20season.

NOTES

NOTES

Made in the USA
Columbia, SC
18 June 2022